"I've worked for almost two decades casting
vision, episodic series, and feature films. Pet...
I hired and trusted to be in rooms with me auditioning and discovering
some of the most talented actors working today. He is not only insightful
and keen with his feedback for actors but is also a nurturing voice of
wisdom and support."

Jandiz Estrada Cardoso, Senior Director,
Global Talent Development, NBC Universal, Los Angeles

"In *Acting for the Camera* Mr. Stone offers a fresh perspective to an age-
old conundrum: how to integrate traditional acting technique with the
demands of the ever-changing, modern acting world. Utilizing easy-
to-understand concepts in a casual, entertaining format, he provides
critical training guideposts to help the emerging actor navigate the oft-
complicated, filmmaking process. Other than persistence, I can't think of
anything more important to an artist with designs on pursuing a professional on-camera career."

Kenneth Suarez, Former Owner - Talent Agent,
Brick Entertainment, Los Angeles

"Peter Allen Stone is a master teacher of acting for the camera. His workshop with our students was incredible! I admire his ability to involve the
students into a fascinating process where all the participants learn by
doing and from each other. I am definitely going to use his book in our
acting for the camera program."

Annemari Untamala, Kallio Upper Secondary School of
Performing Arts, Helsinki, Finland

"Peter Allen Stone's workshops are inspiring and produce clear results
with actors of all levels. He is a master teacher who gets the most out of
an actor's performance, combined with an in-depth knowledge of filmmaking. I have seen him take beginning and professional actors from all
over the world and deliver amazing performances in just four weeks. His
passion and simplistic approach are a rare and effective combination!"

Diana Santi, Film Director, New York Film Academy Florence,
Italy, Program Director

"I am so thankful that I studied with Peter Allen Stone. Beyond his vast knowledge of acting in front of the camera, whether that's involving intricate techniques or tips to enhance your performance, Peter gives you something that cannot be easily taught; he inspires you to be a better human being. He encourages you to relentlessly pursue your passion and pour every bit of yourself into the art form you so dearly love."

Avkash Mann, Vocal Artist, Actor, India

Acting for the Camera

Acting for the Camera: Back to One is a "how to" book with practical steps to achieve a professional performance on camera.

The book focuses on four distinct areas: how to prepare the character, how to execute the technical responsibilities that will assist the editor in creating the on-camera performance in post-production, tips from industry professionals, and how to create effective self-tape auditions. *Part One: The Character's World* is packed with tools with which to analyze the script and fully prepare the character before arriving on set. *Part Two: The Actor's World* focuses on developing technical acting skills for the camera that assist the pre- and post-production teams to create a dynamic on-screen performance. In *Part Three: The Professional World*, industry professionals provide tips from inside the film/TV audition room and how to navigate a career in the acting business. The final section, *Part Four: Self-Tape Like a Pro*, outlines how to build a self-tape studio in the privacy of your own home and submit high-quality self-tape auditions that will help you stand out.

Written for students enrolled in Acting for the Camera courses, *Acting for the Camera: Back to One* explores techniques that can be practiced and mastered by actors of all levels, from the moment they audition for the part through to when they hear the director call "cut!"

Peter Allen Stone is the Head of Acting at the University of Kentucky Department of Theatre and Dance and the former Chair of Acting for Film at the New York Film Academy in New York City. He has worked as an actor in film, television, and theatre, and he assisted as an audition reader for feature films and television at Mackey Sandrich Casting in New York City. He has trained students who have appeared on Broadway, Off-Broadway, in Hollywood and Bollywood films, and on many popular television shows.

Acting for the Camera

Back to One

Peter Allen Stone

Routledge
Taylor & Francis Group

NEW YORK AND LONDON

First published 2021
by Routledge
52 Vanderbilt Avenue, New York, NY 10017

and by Routledge
2 Park Square, Milton Park, Abingdon, Oxon OX14 4RN

Routledge is an imprint of the Taylor & Francis Group, an informa business

© 2021 Peter Allen Stone
Illustrations © 2021 John James Hickey

The right of Peter Allen Stone to be identified as author of this work
has been asserted by him in accordance with sections 77 and 78 of the
Copyright, Designs and Patents Act 1988.

Library of Congress Cataloging-in-Publication Data
Names: Stone, Peter Allen, author.
Title: Acting for the camera: back to one / Peter Allen Stone.
Description: New York, NY: Routledge, 2021. | Includes index.
Identifiers: LCCN 2020052441 (print) | LCCN 2020052442 (ebook) |
ISBN 9780367497682 (hardback) | ISBN 9780367500726 (paperback) |
ISBN 9781003048671 (ebook)
Subjects: LCSH: Motion picture acting. | Television acting. |
Acting–Auditions. | Acting–Vocational guidance.
Classification: LCC PN1995.9.A26 S76 2021 (print) |
LCC PN1995.9.A26 (ebook) | DDC 791.4302/8–dc23
LC record available at https://lccn.loc.gov/2020052441
LC ebook record available at https://lccn.loc.gov/2020052442

ISBN: 978-0-367-49768-2 (hbk)
ISBN: 978-0-367-50072-6 (pbk)
ISBN: 978-1-003-04867-1 (ebk)

Typeset in Adobe Caslon Pro
by Newgen Publishing UK

This book is dedicated to my good friend Dr. Baron Kelly,
who has guided me every step of the way.

CONTENTS

ACKNOWLEDGMENTS

I am fortunate to have had so many incredible teachers, colleagues, and students who have inspired me and supported my work. I want to take this opportunity to thank them for the valuable role they have played.

Thank you to my parents who know nothing about acting but always supported me. Having you say, "We don't know how to help you, but we believe in you" has been the greatest gift that many are not lucky enough to have.

Thank you to my teachers who have inspired and taught me about being an artist: Peter Zapp, Linda Bisesti, Sully White, Meredith McDonough, Michael Dixon, Jon Jory, Melissa Smith, Gregory Wallace, Jeff Crockett, Kevin Jackson, Deborah Sussel, Marco Barricelli, Leslie Felbain, Steven Anthony Jones, Peter Maleitzke, and Frank Ottiwell.

Thank you to my team in New York for giving me opportunity, experience, and support: Jandiz Estrada Cardoso, David Krasner, Ben Sands, Amanda Mackey, Adam Ludwig, Michael James Leslie, Nicholas J. Coleman, Jamie Carroll, Tony Speciale, Glenn Kalison, Tiffany Smile, and Jimonn Cole.

Thank you to the New York Film Academy where I learned from so many incredible artists about acting for the camera: Michael Young, David Klein, Diana Santi, Paul Warner, Lanre Olabisi, Piero Basso AIC,

Glynis Rigsby, Claude Kerven, Giuseppe De Angelis, Benjamin Sidney, and Sean Robinson.

Thank you to my team in Los Angeles for your advice and support: David Denman, Mercedes Masohn, Lindsay Allbaugh, Bettina Niedermann, Carollyn DeVore, and Heather Haase.

Thank you to the University of Kentucky Department of Theatre and Dance for your support.

Thank you to Nidra Sous la Terre, Jandiz Estrada Cardoso, Nelson Henderson, Kenneth Suarez, Jason Liles, and Stacy Solodkin for sharing your expertise and stories.

Thank you to my talented editor and illustrator, John James Hickey, for your encouragement and guidance for an entire year. I am grateful for all of your help.

And, thank you to my students for bringing your imagination, sense of play, and empathy to the work. This book would not exist without you.

Peter Allen Stone

INTRODUCTION

Why *Back to One? Back to one* is an instruction given by the assistant director for the actors and crew to return to their original starting positions at the top of the scene to roll another take. This book uses *Back to One* as a reminder that you must always go *back to the basics* when preparing a role, and *back to yourself* when acting for the camera. It is aimed to inspire you to take ownership of your work and use the camera as a tool to craft your performance. You are the one that is in the frame, the focus is on you, and you want to make every second count.

Acting for the Camera: Back to One is designed for actors who want to develop skills that will improve their performance on camera, and for teachers who want to empower their students. The idea for this book began over 10 years ago and has been developed with the help of many actors, directors, cinematographers, and editors. What makes it unique is that, instead of only focusing on the actor's point of view, *Back to One* addresses the technical skills needed in performance to assist all the artists involved in creating a project. For years, I did research with professional directors, cinematographers, lighting technicians, assistant directors, assistant camera operators, boom operators, sound mixers, and editors. I began with one simple question to each of them, "*How can the actor make their on-camera performance better?*" I listened to them as they described the technical mistakes that actors often make that affect the performance.

Many of them uttered the phrases, "I wish that someone would teach actors this …" or, "If the actor only knew how much it impacts their performance when they do this …" I collected all of their insightful tips and developed exercises that addressed each of their concerns. *Acting for the Camera: Back to One* was born.

Part One: The Character's World focuses on the preparation you must do before you arrive on set. It provides you with tools to analyze the script and create an exciting performance that serves the story. It examines performances from accomplished actors in major film and television shows that support the lesson in each chapter. It outlines how to break down the script and ask useful questions during the creative process that will bring the character to life.

Part Two: The Actor's World concentrates on the technical skills necessary to create a dynamic performance on camera. Each chapter provides a specific exercise to address a technical aspect of acting for the camera. It shows you how to extract clues from the script, helping you create a performance that gives the editor options in post-production. It is important to remember that every technical skill can be mastered through repetition and must be combined with the spontaneous emotional life of the character.

Part Three: The Professional World addresses the actor who wants to pursue a career working in the profession. It takes you inside the audition room of feature films and provides tips from actual auditions of award-winning actors. It introduces the importance of building a professional relationship with the casting director and how to shift your attention to a winning mindset. It encourages you to develop specific goals when auditioning that focus on doing your best work and not just wanting the job. You will receive valuable insight through a series of interviews with professional actors, talent agents, and an award-winning casting director.

Part Four: Self-Tape Like a Pro guides you on how to build your own self-tape studio and submit auditions at a professional level. Today's actor is living in an exciting time and has more access than ever before. Actors are submitting their own self-tape auditions and creating original shows on multiple online platforms. Because they have access to technology, actors can have their projects seen and heard all over the world from their own living room. However, the modern actor must acquire basic skills in lighting, sound, operating the camera, and editing to pursue a career. This section will empower you to be a creator and design the career that aligns with your aspirations.

One final mention. With the aim of inclusivity, I have elected to use the universal term actor and the pronouns they/them when speaking in general.

Now, let's get started and go *Back to One*!

PART ONE
THE CHARACTER'S WORLD

1
PREPARATION

The world of film and television moves quicker than work in the theatre. In the theatre, you have the luxury of weeks of rehearsal to build your character with the director and find a rhythm with your fellow actors. Film and television work at a faster pace. When you are a day player or playing a supporting character, usually you will get a quick blocking rehearsal and maybe a short discussion with the director about an important moment in the scene. Of course, it depends on the size of your role and the production, but don't assume that you will rehearse the scene over and over with the director and the other actors. You must prepare at home and arrive on set ready to shoot.

I will never forget my first television experience, acting in a scene with two of the show's main stars. After arriving on set early in the morning to get into wardrobe and make-up, I waited for hours in my dressing room, running over my lines. When I was finally called to set, the director quickly gave me my blocking. As I ran through a blocking rehearsal with the main actors, I gave my best performance, while they simply marked their performance. They were pros, and it was clear that I was not. Moments before we shot the scene, the director shouted out last-second instructions to the crew as they quickly moved equipment around us. Suddenly, someone from the wardrobe department grabbed me and told me they had to change my shirt because the producer didn't think it suited my character. I darted around a corner and changed my shirt at lightning speed. I didn't want to hold up the production. Adrenaline coursing through my veins, I hurried back to my first mark. Moments before "Action!" was called, I reached out my hand to introduce myself to the other actors. I thought if I connected with them, it would settle my nerves. It did... a little. Our introductions were interrupted by the loud singular voice of the 1st assistant director (AD).

AD: Last looks, everyone.
HAIR/MAKE-UP/WARDROBE: Final touches done.
AD: Cameras ready?
CAMERAS: Ready.
AD: Okay, picture's up! Quiet on set, everybody! Roll sound!
SOUND: Speeding!
AD: Roll camera!
CAMERA: Rolling!
AD: Let's mark it!
2ND AC: This is 37Apple, Take 1. A, B, C, and X Common Mark! (*whacking the slate*)
CAMERA: Camera set!
AD: Okay here we go! Let's settle ...
   (*long silence*)
ME: (*nervous breath ... nervous breath ... nervous breath ...*)
DIRECTOR: And ... Action!

My heart was pounding with excitement, and just like that – we were shooting the scene.

Then, it happened. We were in the middle of the scene, and my mind went completely blank. For some reason, I couldn't remember my next line. I had acted in the theatre for years, but never on camera. This was a new world for me. In that moment where I lost focus, I realized that acting for the camera wasn't as easy as the people on the screen made it look. I stood there internally pleading for the line to come back to me, but it didn't. The director shouted, "Cut! Okay everybody, let's go back to one!" While everyone reset, I stood there for a painful moment thinking my career was over before it began. As I went back to my first position, I took a deep breath, and tried to refocus my energy. Then, the lead actor smiled at me and whispered, "Hey, we got this." I can't thank him enough for his support that day. His small gesture meant the world to me. And then it hit me: we were all on the same team. In fact, everyone on that set was on the same team focusing on their specific job. I began to relax. The 1st AD called the roll again, the director shouted, "Action," and this time, we made it through to the end of the scene. Suddenly, I was an actor on television.

When the episode aired, my friends and family back home congratulated me on how my performance looked natural. Natural? I appreciated their support, but all I could think about was the whirlwind that I had experienced on that day. The atmosphere on a set is filled with energy, and it can be a challenge to focus. I learned a few lessons that day when I stumbled. I learned that what happened to me, happens to many actors. I learned that it didn't ruin my career. And, most importantly, I learned that you must thoroughly prepare the character before you take one step on the set. You have to be ready.

The following chapters in Part One: The Character's World will provide you with a process to analyze your script so that you can play your character with confidence. This process, based on the teachings of Konstantin Stanislavski, is one that I have found effective for myself and my students. When you have been given the honor to give a voice to a character and tell their story, there is no room for thoughts like, "I wish that I had prepared a little more here … If only I had analyzed that moment there … How did I overlook that?" These chapters contain techniques that will not only help you avoid having those thoughts on set, but they will also provide you with a structure to give you confidence when the cameras begin to roll.

2

BREAKING DOWN THE SCRIPT
THE VALUE OF BEATS

What Is a Beat?

Well, it depends on which book you read. Although there are many interpretations of beats, the good news is that they're all correct. In script analysis, a beat is a subdivision of a scene. There are three different ways that you can divide a scene into beats. The first approach is to subdivide a scene by the entrances and exits of the characters. These subdivisions are known as *French scenes*. The second tactic is to subdivide the scene whenever the action changes. For example, *Betty slaps him in the face and walks out of the room.* This particular stage direction has two actions: slapping and exiting. However, the approach that I have found most useful is a third method: breaking down a scene into beats where the topic or subject changes[1]. Each topic shift, whether in the text or the subtext, signals the start of a new beat. This way, the characters can be in the same beat, but they can play their own actions within the beat (see Chapter 6).

But a beat change is not always from your character's point of view or based on the intention of your character. When you mark your beats in your script, step outside of the situation and analyze them from a director's perspective. Ask yourself, "What are these characters talking about?" Are they talking about their favorite food to eat? Are they deciding where they should go on vacation? Are they discussing getting married? Take a look at the television scene below and notice where the beats change. You will see that I have given names to each beat in quotations on the right side of the page.

Scene 2.1

SCENE H

INT. CAFÉ ROSÉ – NIGHT

CHARACTER A AND CHARACTER B HAVE JUST FINISHED THEIR MEAL. CHARACTER A THROWS A FIFTY DOLLAR BILL ON THE TABLE.

"Who's Driving?"

CHARACTER A
Let's go. I'll drive.

CHARACTER B
Why do you always have to drive? I can drive.

CHARACTER A
Come on, we're going to be late. I'm driving!

"The Divorce"

CHARACTER B
I can't do this anymore. I want a divorce.

CHARACTER A
What?

CHARACTER B
You heard me. I've wanted one for a long time.

CHARACTER A
Well, I'm not giving you a divorce.

THEY STARE AT EACH OTHER FOR A MOMENT.

"The Money"

CHARACTER A

(CONT'D)

I didn't mean to lose the money.

CHARACTER B

How could you take our savings without telling me?

CHARACTER A

I made a mistake. I feel horrible.

CHARACTER B

You should.

End of scene.

There are three beats or subjects being discussed in this short scene: *Who's Driving?*, *The Divorce*, and *The Money*. The start of the second beat is when the topic of discussion has shifted from driving to divorce. When the topic of discussion shifted from divorce to money, it creates a third beat. Within each beat, the actor can choose one or more action verbs (see Chapter 6) to play on their scene partner to shape their perform- ance. For example, in the last beat (*"The Money"*), Character A may choose *to beg softly*, with compassion, on their first line, "I didn't mean to lose the money." And when that doesn't stop Character B's inquiry about the money, they may choose a stronger action verb such as *to attack* for their line, "I made a mistake. I feel horrible." However, Character B may choose to play *to demean* for both of their lines. This allows the beat to have a crackling pulse of energy. And when this beat is strung together with the other beats, the entire scene comes alive.

Many years ago, when I lived in Los Angeles, every morning I would go to a coffee shop on Melrose Avenue. Often, I would hear the conversations of the people sitting next to me. It was during that time that I really began to understand what beats were, and how we speak in beats naturally in our everyday life. The next time you are in a coffee shop, casually eavesdrop on a conversation at the next table. You will clearly hear when the topics change, because you are outside of the situation. Make it a game and count their topics or beats. Watch a scene on your favorite television show and see if you can identify the beat changes. This is a great way to practice breaking your scenes into beats. When we step outside of a situation, we can often see it more clearly.

A Screenwriter's Beat

Breaking your scene into beats is different than a *beat* marked by the screenwriter, which is written as a stage direction in parentheses (also known as a wryly). These kinds of *beats* appear in between lines and are used to indicate a pause where a character experiences a shift in thought or emotion.

> MADISON
> I would love to go to your party!
> (beat)
> Oh, you meant as a caterer.

We will discuss in Chapter 12, Art of the Reaction, how to make the most of your performance on camera by using these *beats* to help the editor.

Identify the Subjects

When you first prepare your scene for acting on camera, start by reading it aloud a few times. Read the entire scene with stage directions so you get a full sense of the screenwriter's intentions. Go into each scene admitting that you know nothing about these characters and their situation. Pretend that you are a detective who has arrived at the scene of a crime looking for clues to figure out what happened. Stand outside of the scene, like you are in that coffee shop, and be curious. Identify what subjects are being discussed. Notice which character changes the subject and why. Are they trying to avoid the subject? If so, why? Are they nervous? Why? Are they trying to stay on the topic that will help them get what they want? This will help you understand your character's intentions and desires.

Name the Beats

Mark and name the beat changes. After you have read the scene multiple times aloud, begin to break it into beats by drawing a line across the page when the subject changes, and on the right side of your script write down a name for each beat (see Scene 2.1 above). Have fun naming the beats as if they were movie titles, but choose names that are associated with the topic being discussed. You want these titles to remind you specifically of what you are talking about. It will help you get clear with your actions. Here are some examples of beat titles: "The Encounter," "The Proposal," "Father Is Sick," "Mom Is a Goddess," "The Cheater," "Wounds Take Time to Heal," and "Drugs Are Bad." It's important to remember that there isn't a "Beat Police" that is going to arrest you for marking your beats in slightly different places than another actor. Breaking your scene into beats is work that you do to help you act the scene. It is your private analysis that will help you map out how you want to play the character before the camera begins to roll.

The Value of Beats

Why should you break your script into beats?

1.   Improves comprehension;
2.   Helps you learn your lines quicker; and
3.   Prevents you from playing the result or end of the scene.

Comprehension

Here is a helpful way to think about beats:

book = screenplay
chapter = scene
paragraph = beat

Using the *book = screenplay* example above, is it easier to analyze a book, a chapter, or a paragraph? Obviously, because of its smaller size, it's easier to analyze a paragraph. The same is true for your work on a script. It is much easier to analyze a beat than a larger scene or the entire screenplay. When you are preparing, imagine that each beat as a mini scene. Looking closely at these smaller segments of the scene will help you to comprehend what specifically is happening between the characters and to not overlook an important moment in the text. We all miss moments in the text if we don't take time to scrutinize the words. Do the work, and it will pay off in your performance.

Learning the Lines

In the world of film and television, you have to learn your scenes quickly, and it is a muscle that you can strengthen with practice. If you are a lucky person that was born with a photographic memory, congratulations! I envy you. Most of us do not have that gift. When you first begin to work on a scene, don't overwhelm yourself with the pressure of learning it all at once. You will surprise yourself how quickly you can memorize a scene if you go one beat at a time. Have a friend rehearse each beat with you and, when you feel confident, move on to the next one until you get to the end of the scene. I have witnessed many actors learn an entire scene in an hour using this technique. This is especially valuable for auditioning when you often have a limited amount of time. Also, it will help you to identify the transitions in the scene. Give it a try and see how quickly you can learn each beat.

Learn the Thought

It is helpful to learn the thought behind each line that your character speaks and not just the lines. Notice that I didn't use the word *memorize*; I used the word *learn*. To help thread your lines together, look for words or actions that give your character the thought to speak their next line. In life, we have thoughts and intentions behind everything that we say. The next time you are having a conversation with a friend, see if you can figure out what your friend says that gives you the impulse to speak. Now, do the same with your script and identify in the scene the words or actions (e.g., *snapping their gum*) that gives your character the thought to speak. Go through your beats and circle the *words* or *actions* that compel you to say your line. Here's an example:

Example 2.1

Characters A and B are in a romantic relationship. What does Character A say that gives Character B the thought to speak?

CHARACTER A

I don't want to lose you. Why won't you tell me that
you love me? I need your support now more than ever.

CHARACTER B

Because you love your career more than me.

Character A's second line, "Why won't you tell me that you love me?"
sparks the thought for Character B to speak their line. If you are playing
Character B, circle the word "*love*" in your script so that your mind will be
reminded of your next line. This will help you learn the thoughts of your
character and not just memorize the lines.

Avoid Playing the Result

Breaking your scene into beats will prevent you from playing the result or
ending of the scene. It's not as interesting to see a volcano that has already
erupted. We want to see the volcano build pressure, begin to shake, vent
hot ash, and then erupt! The same goes for playing a scene on camera.
We want to see your character pursue their need, struggle, and evolve.
We want to see a character that is trying to hold their emotions together
and not just sitting there in a puddle of tears. It is compelling to watch
a character that is trying their best to contain their emotions without
crying. The most exciting acting occurs when the character is on the verge
of crumbling but tries to keep it together. No matter how long or short
the scene is, give yourself room to grow. Study the last beat of the scene
to see where your character ends, and then make sure that you start the
first beat in a different emotional place.

One of my favorite actors is Viola Davis. Her performances are the
perfect combination of heart and technique. And she allows her emotion
to fuel the action of the story. In the 2016 movie *Fences*[2], based on the
play by August Wilson, she plays Rose opposite Denzel Washington's
Troy. There is a heartbreaking scene at the end of the movie when Troy
reveals to his wife that he has been having an affair and impregnated
another woman. Rose confronts Troy and expresses the sacrifices that
she has made for years throughout their marriage. She deserves better,
and she tells him. The scene is powerful because Ms. Davis provides

a wonderful example of an actor not playing the result or end of the scene. She begins the scene with her hands behind her back and her head slightly down. She has been betrayed by her husband. She says her first line with a soft voice. You can see that she is emotionally shaken. The fire is burning inside of her, but she contains it. Throughout the scene, the emotion inside her builds and builds until the volcano *has* to erupt, because she cannot contain it any longer. We sit on the edge of ours seats, waiting with anticipation to see if and when she will explode. And when she does, you can't take your eyes off of her. Brilliant acting. It's not surprising that Viola Davis won the Academy Award for Best Supporting Actress for her performance.

Chapter Notes

- Beats are a change in subject between the characters.
- Break your scene into beats by drawing a line across the page.
- Name your beats on the right side of the page.
- Beats are helpful for comprehension, learning lines, and not playing the ending of the scene.
- Book = screenplay; chapter = scene; paragraph = beat.
- Learn your scene beat by beat.
- Learn the character's thoughts and not just the lines.
- Circle the words or actions that spark the thought for your next line.

3

GIVEN CIRCUMSTANCES AND RELATIONSHIPS

BRING LIFE ON

Given circumstances are the facts given to you by the screenwriter[1]. If the script says that your character is sitting in the kitchen at three o'clock in the afternoon, then you must play those circumstances. You need to make us believe that you are sitting in the kitchen at three o'clock in the afternoon, even if, in reality, you are shooting at two o'clock in the morning. If the script says that your character just went through a divorce or has just won $100,000 in the lottery, then you must allow those circumstances to affect your character, because you are in service of the story. You want to go through your script and make a list of all the facts that you can find about the situation and your character. It will be helpful to identify as many aspects of your character as possible, such as their: age, social status, religion, political views, profession, relationship status, family, and gender identity. This is not a complete list, but it's a place to start. Imagine if an actor were playing you. Think of all the things that they could write down that make you unique. Once you can begin to see the character as a real person, you will be inspired to fill them with your imagination.

Bringing Life to Your Character

Often, given circumstances can be small, but they are just as important. Imagine that you are playing the role of a hotel concierge in the drama miniseries *The Queen's Gambit*, and your line is, "Good morning. I have a package for you. Will you please sign?" What is happening to your character right before you say your line? What is your character thinking about? Where is their attention? It shouldn't be an earth-shattering circumstance that doesn't make any sense or isn't supported by the script. Think about your character's profession, social status, and/or relationship to that other character. Even in a supporting role, you need to analyze the script and look for any clues that will help you to bring life to your character.

Characters, like people, do not appear out of thin air. Each character has their own back story (who they are and where they come from). They have a set of circumstances that have happened prior to the beginning of the scene. These circumstances will inform you how the character may act or react in a given moment. Therefore, it is essential that you make a choice about what is happening with your character just before they say their first line of dialogue in the scene. This will help you relax, because you will be focusing on something other than yourself. Look closely at your script and make a choice about the energy that your character is bringing into the scene.

Clearly identifying the given circumstances in the script will give you a foundation to build an exciting performance. It will ignite your imagination and inspire you to play the scene. Go through your beats and make a list of every fact that you discover in the scene. Film and television shows are often shot out of order, and, therefore, it is essential that you map out the life of your character scene by scene.

A wonderful example of an actor bringing the life of the character into the scene is Geena Davis in the film *Thelma and Louise*[2], starring Susan Sarandon and a young Brad Pitt. This is an incredible buddy road film that is considered a classic. *Thelma and Louise* received six Academy Award nominations, and both Sarandon and Davis were nominated for Best Actress. Thelma (played by Davis) and Louise (played by Sarandon) are on the run, driving across the country after Louise has shot and killed a man who was attempting to rape Thelma outside a bar. On the road, they come across a young cowboy drifter, J.D. (played by Pitt). Thelma quickly falls for him and convinces Louise to let him hitch a ride with them. Thelma and J.D. have just had a passionate, romantic night together at the hotel, and the next morning Louise waits for Thelma at the diner. Louise is seated at a table, and Thelma strolls across the restaurant to join her. Her hair is messed up, she giggles, and her body sways as she walks. Finally, she plops down into the booth with an enormous smile across her face. She is slightly out of breath, and her eyes are glazed over like she has just had the greatest night of her life. As she tells Louise about her romantic night, she plays the scene with excitement, like a champagne bottle that is about to pop. Geena Davis is fearless with her bold choices that support the given circumstances of the script. The romantic encounter that her character has just had with J.D. was likely shot on an entirely different day. This is the work of a professional actor who has studied the script in detail and is bringing on a character that is full of life.

Relationships

It is important to be clear on how your character feels about the other character and how they feel about themselves. What is their opinion about the other character in the scene? Is your character higher or lower status than the other character? If they are lower status, are they trying to gain a higher status? In *Thelma and Louise*, Louise usually has the higher status. In the early parts of the film, Thelma is always looking to her for the answers. Louise literally drives the car and she makes the important decisions. However, the status changes throughout the film when Thelma begins to take more action. Analyze your script and identify the status of your character for each scene. Notice when your character has a higher or lower status. How do they feel about themselves? Do they take charge? Or do they allow others to lead? In life, our status changes quickly depending on whom we encounter. The same needs to be true for the character you are playing.

Make It Your Own

You must always fill the character with your artistic point of view. You have been hired to play the role, and we want to see your version of the character. Combine the given circumstances with your imagination and make the character your own. This makes acting much more fun

Scene 3.1

INT. BARGAIN CAR RENTAL – DAY

CHARACTER A and CHARACTER B approach the counter in a busy and crowded office. The ASSISTANT MANAGER quickly approaches.

ASSISTANT MANAGER
Welcome to Bargain Car Rental! May I help you?

CHARACTER B
Sure, if someone remembers where they put the money.

CHARACTER A
Would you quit acting like this in public?

ASSISTANT MANAGER
(beat)
I'll be right with you … after I make this phone call.

End of scene.

Headings and Action Descriptions

Always pay attention to each scene heading and description of the action that follows, because they are packed with useful clues. Scene headings in film and television scripts will contain three main parts in the scene heading:

1. An interior or exterior indicator (INT. or EXT.)
2. Scene locator (e.g., BARGAIN CAR RENTAL), and
3. Time (DAY or NIGHT).

The example above lets us know that we are *inside* a *bargain car rental* office during the *day*.

The action description, which follows the scene heading, will tell you who is in the scene as well as giving descriptive words about the physical setting and the atmosphere. Using the example above and combining what we know from the scene heading (time and place) with the action description, we are presented with a series of descriptive words (*day*, *busy*, *crowded*, and *quickly)* that help us to understand the situation. Allow these circumstances to spark your imagination and create a believable character.

Let's imagine that you are preparing the role of the Assistant Manager. What facts does the screenwriter give you? How does this spark your imagination? It's a short scene, but there are clues that can help you make strong choices and add life to the character.

Given Circumstances – Facts

- You are in a car rental office.
- It is daytime.
- You are the Assistant Manager.
- The office is busy and crowded.
- You attempt to take help them.
- Characters A and B are having an argument.
- You leave to answer the phone.

How can you take this information, combine it with your imagination, and make a choice about the life that you bring before your first line of dialogue? Here are a few questions to ask:

Questions and Answers

- What do managers in a business usually want?
  They want their customers to have a good experience and tell others about the company.
- How does the scene end for the Assistant Manager?
  Probably awkwardly and uncomfortably, because the two begin to have an argument in front of a complete stranger in a place of business. If it ends awkwardly for your character, then a strong choice would be to play the opposite at the top of the scene to give your character a journey.
- The script says that the office is *crowded*. What type of energy could your character bring into the scene?
  It would be logical to play that you are moving quickly doing a bunch of tasks, slightly out of breath and trying to remain calm.

- The Assistant Manager does not know the customers.
  If the Assistant Manager knew the customers, they would be addressed by their names. They are strangers, but the Assistant Manager gives the customers a higher status because the Assistant Manager wants to serve them.

So, based on the given circumstances (facts) and your imagination, you could bring the following life to your performance:

You arrive at the counter slightly out of breath. You smile at them because you want them to have a good experience and begin to help them with a positive spirit.

How Do You Do It?

Now, you've made a choice based on the given circumstances and your imagination, but how do you do it? How can you prepare yourself to arrive at the counter, slightly out of breath, and make it believable? Here is one way. Right before the director calls action, do some quick physical movements off camera to get your body engaged. You could quickly run in place or hop up and down a few times. Now, when you arrive at the counter, you will be connected to your body and a little out of breath. You will be creating the reality of an assistant manager in a busy office and bringing on the life of the character. Keep it subtle and don't worry about looking ridiculous. You are doing the work of an actor. You are getting your body engaged so that the camera will believe that you are the character and not an actor on a set.

Go to YouTube and watch legendary actor Jack Nicholson prep[3] for his famous axe scene in the classic psychological horror film *The Shining*[4], directed by Stanley Kubrick. In a climactic scene, Nicholson's character (Jack Torrance) has become deranged, and he uses an axe to hack his way through the bathroom door where his wife, Wendy, played by Shelly Duvall, is hiding. During Nicholson's quick preparation, you can see him run in little circles, jumping up and down with the axe in his hands. The crew pays no attention and moves around him as they get ready for the shot. He is prepping physically and emotionally for the intensity he needs when he hacks through door with the axe. When he arrives at the door, he is slightly out of breath, his body is alive, and he has a crazed look in his eyes. If you haven't already, watch these masterful performances by Nicholson and Duvall. Observe their scenes closely and notice the specific life that they are bringing at the start of each scene. So, even when performing an intense role, find a sense of play to get you in the right physical and emotional place to begin the scene.

Chapter Notes

- Given circumstances are facts that are given by the screenwriter.
- Combine the given circumstances with your imagination to make your choices.
- Bring life to your character.
- Characters come from a specific place.
- Look for clues that will help you play the scene.
- Pay attention to the scene headings and description of action.
- Start the scene in a different emotional place than the ending.

4

OBJECTIVE

MAKE IT ABOUT THE OTHER CHARACTER

An objective is what your character wants from the other character in the scene. Objectives come naturally to us in life. Think about how often you walk into a situation with a family member, colleague, or romantic partner, and you want something from them. By the way, this does not make you a bad person, but it does make you a human being. Daily, we pursue simple objectives such as getting up in the morning, eating breakfast, or exercising before we go to work. We pursue larger objectives such as wanting to nail that audition, ace the final exam, or marry the love of our life. Big or small, our days are filled with objectives that we play. As an exercise, write down the objectives that you play throughout the day. You may be surprised at the number of things that you want. Also, write down the things that people want from you in an average day. If you make it your objective to notice other people's objectives, you will be amazed to see how many goals we pursue each day.

Make It About the Other Character

What do you want from the other character? This is a question that must always be answered, and it is not a time to be general, philosophical, or too intellectual. What your character wants in the scene should be direct and always in relation to the other character. Challenge yourself to answer this question in one sentence and try to avoid using fancy words. A strong objective is visceral and fueled by desire. Choose an objective that stirs your emotions and inspires you to play the scene.

Here are some examples of objectives. Imagine that you need to get your spouse to sign the divorce papers. Or you've been hit with unexpected medical expenses and you want a raise from your grumpy boss. Or, you want to get your friend to help you build an actor website for you before you meet with a big agent. (Not a bad idea, by the way.) The same is true for the character that you are playing. What do you want from the other character in the scene? This question is not merely acting jargon or an academic exercise. The answer to that question will give your character a purpose. Playing an objective that serves the story will improve your acting instantly. Acting becomes much easier when you know what you're doing, what you want, and what you are willing to do (your action) to get it. The answers to these questions will guide you in performance. I often hear actors say, "Yes, I know what an objective is; I've have learned that already." Knowing and demonstrating are two different things. Reciting the definition of an objective is an easy assignment, but playing one effectively takes practice and effort.

Emotional Stakes

What are the emotional stakes for your character's objective? How important is it for your character to get what they want now? It is helpful to focus on the *why* behind the *what* for your character's objective. After you select your objective, ask yourself why, to find the reason that powers the objective. You want to pick an objective that ignites you and sparks the emotional life of the character. It will not help you if you choose passive objectives that have no emotional impact. A way to test your objective is to ask yourself, "Does it matter if my character gets this objective now?" How will they feel if they don't get it? Good screenwriters crank up the dial on the emotional stakes for the character. Your job is to select an objective that serves the story and raises the emotional needs for the character. In a comedy or a drama, if your objective is packed with emotion, it will be compelling to watch.

Play to Win

Scenes are always stronger when the actor/character plays to win. The screenwriter decides if your character achieves their objective in the scene, but the actor/character should always play to win. It's uninteresting to watch a character who easily gives up on their objective. For example, if a character gets dumped by their partner, it's unexciting to see them grovel in their own despair for an entire scene. It's wonderful if they are emotionally affected, but an audience wants to watch them fight for them and try to win them back. Always channel the emotion that your character is feeling and allow it to fuel your objective. In the example, the screenwriter may choose to end the scene with the character not achieving their objective. That could be a powerful and fascinating scene. However, it will be even more impactful if you play to win.

Scene Objectives versus Super Objectives

The scene objective is what you want from the other character within the scene. The super objective is what your character is pursuing throughout the entire script. Your super objective is the sum total of all of your character's scene objectives. I find it helpful to visualize a tree when I think of objectives versus super objectives. The super objective is the trunk of the tree that supports all of the branches or scene objectives. The branches (scene objectives) feed into the trunk, which is your character's overall mission in the script. You can also think of it as a large staircase. Each step represents a scene objective, and at the top you will find your super objective.

A wonderful example of great acting and strong character objectives is in the 2014 movie *Whiplash*[1], starring Miles Teller and J.K. Simmons. The movie is about an ambitious jazz drummer named Andrew and his abusive teacher, Terrence Fletcher. The main theme of the movie asks the question, "How far should you go to be great, and what happens when you cross that line?" The movie is incredible, and it shows how important an objective can be when it is fueled with emotion. The stakes of Andrew's objective are very high. This makes his character compelling to watch. We root for him to win and achieve his goal. Andrew's super objective is simple and direct: *to be the greatest jazz drummer of all time.*

Throughout the film, he pursues this super objective at all costs, including risking his own life. There is nothing, and I mean nothing, that he won't do to achieve this dream. In the first scene, we see Andrew drumming alone at night, when he is suddenly approached by the famous teacher. In this short scene, Fletcher asserts his authority and tests Andrew's abilities. A nervous Andrew bangs on his drums and plays his heart out for Fletcher. He tries to impress him and be accepted. Andrew's objective in this scene is simple: *to win Fletcher's approval*. He doesn't achieve his objective in this scene, but he pursues it with all of his heart. Always play to win. The audience wants to see you go after your goal, even if the character comes up short.

Make It Simple

Choose an objective that is supported by the text, inspires you to act, and connected to the emotional needs of your character. Do not complicate things by trying to play an objective that is too broad. This may make you self-conscious, and your performance will be general. Keep your objective direct and simple. You should be able to say it in one sentence, and *always make the objective about the other character in the scene*. It is not about you; it is about what you want from them.

I want to be loved is a weak objective because it is abstract, general, and directionless. *I want my mother to accept my love* is a much stronger objective because it involves the other character. That is an objective that you can play. *I want to be left alone* is a weak objective because it only involves you. This choice puts your character on an island by themselves. *I want my boyfriend to leave the room because he betrayed me* is exciting to watch and loaded with drama. When you involve the other character with your objective, the audience will lean forward.

How Do You Identify the Objective?

A helpful way to find your character's objective is to look at the end of the scene. Analyze the last couple of beats of the scene and you will find your answer. What is your character saying? What is your character doing? What is your character trying to get from the other character in the final moments? When you identify this, your objective will appear.

Another helpful tool in finding your character's objective is to identify the other character's objective first. Have you ever noticed that, in life, it is sometimes easier to help a friend deal with a problem than it is to help yourself with a similar one? Stepping outside of the situation and analyzing the other character's objective will provide clarity. Study the other character and figure out what they're trying to get from you. The characters' objectives should be in conflict with each other. Identify their objective and choose an objective for your character that is in opposition. It is like soccer: nobody would pay to watch a match where both teams are trying to score the ball in the same goal.

It's Like a Flower: Give It Room to Grow

Give your character an opportunity to go on a journey in the scene. Where in the scene does the objective become clear? Examine the beats and look for the moments where your objective begins to poke its head out. The more slowly you reveal your objective, the more interesting your performance will be to watch. You don't want the audience to know exactly where your character is going from the start. If the audience gets ahead of you, the scene dies. Bring the audience along for the ride and don't let them arrive at the end before your character. Think of your objective at the beginning of the scene as a little seed that has been planted. It is small and difficult to see, but it is there … growing beat by beat. By the end of the scene, your objective has broken through the soil, sprouted, and is in full bloom.

Chapter Notes

- An objective is what your character wants from the other character in the scene.
- Always make it about the other character.
- Find the reason why the objective is important to your character.
- A super objective is what your character wants overall in the story.
- Choose an objective that is direct and simple and stirs your emotions.
- Identify the other character's objective and look at the end of the scene to find your objective.
- Give your objective room to grow.

5

OBSTACLES
CHARACTER PROBLEMS ARE ACTOR GIFTS

An obstacle is anything that stands in the way of your character getting what they want. Most of the time, the obstacles will be provided by the other character in the scene. If the writing is good, the other character's need will make it difficult for your character to get what they want. It's important to identify the obstacles and attempt to overcome them as you pursue your character's objective. If you examine the scene closely, you will find obstacles that come from your character's internal struggles and, often, the location where the scene takes place. For example, your character's objective may be to ace their final exam, but, owing to past experiences, they suffer from anxiety when performing under pressure. This is an internal obstacle that may stand in the way of your character achieving their objective. Or, perhaps your character wants to get their romantic partner to apologize for being rude at dinner, but the scene takes place in the orchestra section of a Broadway play during a performance. These obstacles are little gifts that the actor must crave.

Character Problems Are Actor Gifts

What are the problems between the characters in the scene? When you begin to work on a scene, it is easy to fall into the trap of wanting to perform right away. You quickly scan through the scene and ask yourself,

"What do I get to say? What do I get to do? What does my character want?" All of these questions are important, but, if you avoid making the problems (obstacles) a large focus of the scene, you will be missing a golden opportunity. Identifying *why* it is difficult for your character to get what they want is essential to good acting.

In my life, I do not seek out conflict and look for problems. I prefer to live my life in peace, and not in a state of constant dramatic conflict. That would be both stressful and exhausting. In acting, the opposite is true. We must dig up the problems, cherish and highlight them. A great Shakespeare teacher once told me, "We go to the circus to watch the tightrope walker fall, not get to the other side." Think about that for a moment. Why do we pay to watch that performer on a rope stretched out across the arena? Because it's exciting, dangerous, and seemingly impossible to do. If we know for a fact that they will easily get to the other side, we won't be interested in watching it. We want to see the struggle. We want to see the performer on the tightrope take a deep breath, attempt to calm their nerves, and wipe the sweat off their brow as they take their dangerous first step. It's a part of human nature to be drawn to a dramatic situation, even if it makes us feel uncomfortable. In acting, we should relish the opportunity to be in a difficult position that we often don't experience in life.

What's the Argument?

Bring out the arguments in every scene that you play. Aaron Sorkin, the brilliant playwright and screenwriter (*A Few Good Men*, *The Social Network*, and *The West Wing*), says he is always the first actor to play a part and, when he is writing, he will talk out loud as the character and start arguments with himself[1]. This is a good reminder about the importance of conflict. When breaking down your scene, ask yourself, "What is the argument that is being discussed?" Go through each beat of your scene and identify the disagreement between the characters. It's not interesting to watch a scene between two characters who agree on everything. Viewers want to see characters who are in opposition to each other as they attempt to achieve their objectives. Of course, embracing the conflict doesn't mean that the characters have to be yelling at each other for the entire scene. Acting is not about who screams the loudest, but sometimes we do raise our voices when the stakes are high. Whether you are acting in a drama, comedy, or horror film, embrace the opportunity to be in conflict with another character and bring out the arguments. Don't avoid the conflict because it's safer. It's a gift given to you by the screenwriter. I promise that it will be exciting to watch and fun to play.

Think about your favorite scenes from movies and television shows. I bet that they are loaded with obstacles, problems, and conflict between the characters. Why can't they get along? How difficult would it be to be in that crazy situation? Comedies are especially filled with huge problems between the characters. The bigger the problem for your character, the bigger the gift for you. An audience loves to watch characters in painful situations. Think about the Academy Award-nominated movie *Bridesmaids*[2]. It's hilarious and loaded with character problems. The main character, Annie, loses her bakery, her boyfriend leaves her, she runs out of money, and has to move in with two roommates ... and that's just the beginning of the movie. Annie runs into one problem after the next that she must confront. When we watch a scene with a lot of conflict, often our impulse is to look away, but we keep watching because we can't help ourselves. Another wonderful example of characters with all kinds of problems is the romantic comedy-drama *Silver Linings Playbook*[3], starring Jennifer Lawrence and Bradley Cooper. This movie is dramatic, touching, hilarious, and loaded with obstacles. The characters deal with a dead spouse, cheating wife, battles with depression, and a bipolar disorder to name a few. In every scene, these actors embrace all of their character's problems by shining a light on them. We feel their pain and cheer them on as they face their struggles. The movie received Academy Award nominations in all of the acting categories, and Jennifer Lawrence took home the statue for Best Actress. If you haven't seen this movie, be sure to watch it and notice how the characters run toward their problems and not away from them.

Chapter Notes

- An obstacle is anything that stands in the way of your character getting what they want.
- Character problems are actor gifts.
- We go to the circus to watch the tightrope walker fall, not get to the other side.
- Search for the obstacles and bring them into the open for all to see.
- Don't run away from the problems; run toward them.

6

ACTIONS
OCEAN VERSUS POND ACTING

The Choice is Yours

Characters are defined by action. Actions reveal to others who we are. They're what you do to get what you want. When an action is played effectively, it can create an emotional response in another character. More importantly, actions are what you, as the character, *choose* to do. The actions you play are your artistic choice and what makes your performance different than anyone else's performance. To act is to take action.

In life, we play actions, subconsciously and consciously, all day long. How do you convince the salesperson at a clothing store to return a sweater without a receipt? Depending on the situation, you may try by charming them or pleading with them. How do you get your friend to have dinner at your favorite restaurant instead of theirs? You may try by getting them excited about the new menu or by guilting them because you ate at their favorite restaurant the last time. The best actors play specific and interesting actions that bring the story to life. The legendary actor and teacher Stella Adler said, "Your talent is in your choice."[1] It's important that you make a choice that excites you and supports the story. Trust your creative impulse, because your interpretation matters. In television, writers often write the character for the actor. So, always bring yourself to the role.

Ocean versus Pond Acting

Great acting flows like an ocean. It does not sit still like water in a pond. In a pond, the water is stagnant and isolated. It has little movement and sits alone. Pond acting is excruciatingly boring to watch because it doesn't involve the other character. Ocean acting ebbs and flows like the tide. It's alive because you are exchanging energy with the other character. Your acting can have the same power that waves have when they crush rocky cliffs or toss a ship at sea, if you play actions that affect your scene partner. Ocean acting enables you to send actions or energy back and forth with your partner. You will create an exciting scene if you power each action with your thoughts, ideas, and emotions. What makes a scene dynamic, and therefore fascinating to watch, is the continuous transfer of that energy back and forth between the characters as they respond to what each other says and does. Great acting occurs when you send energy to the other character, receive their energy, and send it back again.

Playable Action Verbs

Actions are playable verbs. To flirt, to attack, to inspect, to guilt, to interrogate, to support, and to challenge are some examples of verbs that you can play. It's important to note that you don't get an award for coming up with the most intellectual verbs. Choose actions that mean something to you and inspire you to act. You can use your own slang or shorthand when you select actions, because, ultimately, they're for you. Another way to think of actions is to ask yourself, "What am I trying to get my partner to understand with this line?" "What do I mean when I say the line?" "What is the subtext or message underneath the line?" Notice if your action lands on them. Did they receive the intention that you sent to them? Did they understand what you meant? Did they get it? Did it affect them? Be specific, but don't overcomplicate choosing your actions. If your objective in a scene is to get your friend to apologize for not inviting you to their engagement party, great, but how are you going to do it? By demanding an apology? Or are you going to make them feel guilty? Some actors believe that, if you select and rehearse your actions before you arrive on set, your performance will become empty and mechanical. I haven't found this to be true. Rehearsing your actions before you shoot the scene will give you freedom in the moment. It will allow you to release the work and be present because you have built a structure to tell the story. The same action is never played exactly the same way twice. Actions can be spontaneous each time that you play them, if you are listening to your partner. One of the big challenges when acting for the camera is to make it appear as if it is happening for the first time with each take. You want your performance to be balanced with spontaneity and consistency. This can be achieved by rehearsing your actions to the point that you don't have to think about them and listening to the other character.

Remove the Shield

When playing a scene, make a conscious choice that you will allow the other character's actions to affect you. It takes courage to be vulnerable, and it will make you a better actor. It's uninteresting to watch a character who has an imaginary shield protecting them and is never affected by the other character. Of course, there are exceptions, and all characters are affected differently. However, sometimes, we can get so focused on our actions and game plan that we forget about what the other character is sending to us. Listen to them, breathe, and open your heart to what they are saying. When you step into a scene with another character, remind yourself that you welcome the other character's actions. You invite their actions to affect you emotionally because it will make the scene more compelling. Avoid being so committed to your character's mission that you forget to receive the thoughts, ideas, and feelings that are being sent to you from the other character. If you approach your work with this mindset, you will be rewarded with exciting and spontaneous moments.

A Scene Is a Piece of Music

A scene is like a piece of music with tempo, tone, rhythm, and texture. Think of the actions like musical notes in a song. If we had to listen to a song that played the same musical note over and over again for 3 minutes straight, we would quickly become bored or annoyed. The same goes for playing a scene. An audience stays engaged by seeing a character play a variety of actions as they pursue their objective. Go through each beat of your scene and ask yourself, "What am I doing to the other character in this section?" Make sure that you aren't playing the same action for the entire scene, because the audience will tune out. Surprise them with variety. You want to always be slightly ahead of the audience and, like a chess player, never let them see where the next move is coming from.

An excellent example of a character using multiple actions to get what they want is in the 1995 film *The Basketball Diaries*[2], starring Leonardo DiCaprio. DiCaprio plays the autobiographical character, Jim Carroll, a promising high school basketball player and writer in New York City, who becomes addicted to heroin. In the film, Jim's mother kicks him out of the house and onto the street. Jim will do anything, including prostitution, to get his fix. At the end of the movie, in one of the most heart-wrenching scenes you will ever see, Jim tries to get $20 from his mom through the chain of their apartment door. His objective is to get the money for his habit. DiCaprio's performance is filled with emotion, and he allows his character to grow in the scene by playing a variety of actions. He begins the scene by making her feel loved, relaxed, and safe. He reaches through the crack of the door and holds his mother's hand, reminding her that he is still her little boy. When she refuses to give him the money, he guilts, begs, threatens, demands, and attacks her with his words. He continues to try new tactics to get what he desperately wants. It is a difficult scene to witness, but a beautiful work of art. When you watch it, notice how DiCaprio doesn't let the volcano erupt until the end. His mom, played brilliantly by Lorraine Bracco, painfully calls the police on her own son and says into the phone, "Officer, someone's breaking into my apartment."

The Unexpected Action

When you are rehearsing, continue to explore many different actions until you find your interpretation of the character. Once you've broken down your script and found actions that motivate you, explore more actions to see what you find. Any time you have the thought, "Well, my character wouldn't do that. That doesn't make any sense. My character would never …," be careful. This may be true, but it may also not be true. For example, your character's objective may be to get the other character to go on a date. The obvious choice would be to make it clear from the start that you are romantically interested in them. However, it may add dimension to the scene if, in the opening beat, you make the other character feel that you are not interested by gently pushing them away as a tactic to achieve your objective. Playing an unexpected action will give your performance depth and make the character more human. When people or characters do something other than what we expect, they are instantly more intriguing. Explore many actions in rehearsal before you commit to your final choices.

Throw the Homework Away!

When you are shooting your scene, throw your homework away. Forget about it! Trust yourself and the preparation that you have done. Analysis time is over. Now, it's time to play. Breathe, look into your partner's eyes, and see what happens. Be receptive to what they are giving you. If you are open and trust the moment, you will receive the greatest gift. Listen to the other character, allow yourself to be affected, and let the ocean flow. Acting is not about being perfect; it's about being present. An unplanned moment can be a golden opportunity for magic to occur. Welcome the unexpected and, no matter what happens when the cameras are rolling, stay in the moment and listen to your partner.

Chapter Notes
- Character is defined by action.
- Act like an ocean not a pond.
- Actions are verbs that help you pursue your objective.
- The actions are your choice.
- Remove the shield and be affected.
- Scenes are like music, with a variety of notes and dynamics.
- Pick actions that excite you.
- Explore many actions before you commit to your choices.
- Throw your homework away.

7

CHARACTER NOTEBOOK
MAPPING OUT THE ROLE

Emotional Continuity

Emotional continuity is the believability of your character, flowing from shot to shot and scene to scene throughout the story. It is not as easy as it sounds, but, if you prepare and practice, you will create a fluid performance. You want your performance to match emotionally with the previous shot and scene and flow naturally. Good emotional continuity on screen should go unnoticed, and the average viewer should never think about your performance emotionally matching. When I see fluid emotional continuity on screen, I applaud the actors, because I know that it's a challenge.

As mentioned earlier in Chapter 3: Given Circumstances and Relationships, movies and television shows are usually shot out of sequential order. There are many reasons for this, but often it's because of money. If the script has two scenes set in a high school, and the production team can reserve that high school on Day 12 of shooting, they'll shoot both scenes on that day to save time and money. What if those two scenes are on pages 8–10 and 64–67 in the script? Hopefully, your character will have changed and evolved between those two scenes. It's important to map out your character's journey so that your performance is fluid and logical. I have a friend who is currently acting on a new TV series, and the production, like most of the world, has been shut down owing to the COVID-19 pandemic. It began as a month-long shoot and now has been extended to an entire year before it will be completed. Obviously, this is a big challenge for everyone involved. Think about the amount of time that will have passed between the shooting of scenes.

Character Notebook

To track your character's journey and emotional continuity, create a character notebook as part of your preparation. Write down detailed notes for each scene in the script. This will help you to see your character's arc and super objective and track their emotional journey. Keep your notebook with you and use your notes as a quick reminder to help you get into character before you shoot each scene. You will be putting your performance at risk if you arrive on set without mapping this out first. Separate each scene in your notebook and answer the character/scene questions (listed below). Also, write down notes after you finish shooting a scene. This will help if a lot of time has passed between your shoot days.

Character's Journey

One of the easiest ways to visualize your character's arc is to map out each scene in sequential order at the beginning of your notebook for quick reference. List your objective for each scene. This will allow you to see your character's super objective and their emotional journey. Make a note of any major events or moments that happen in the scenes. This will help you to create a fluid performance even when the scenes are shot out of sequential order.

Character's Journey

Scene 1 (p. 1) – INT./EXT – LOCATION – DAY/NIGHT
Scene objective

Scene 2 (p. 3) – INT./EXT – LOCATION – DAY/NIGHT
Scene objective

Scene 3 (p. 7) – INT./EXT – LOCATION – DAY/NIGHT
Scene objective

Scene 67 (p. 94) – INT./EXT – LOCATION – DAY/NIGHT
Scene objective

Character/Scene Questions (from Your Character's Point of View)

Give yourself adequate time to think about these questions. There is no need to rush. Take your character for a walk, listen to music that helps you connect to your character, and daydream. Answer the questions in detail and read them over before you shoot your scene to remind yourself what has happened and what is happening right now. Sit in your dressing room, close your eyes, and imagine the world of your character. Your character notebook is private. It is only for you. Keep it with you when you are on set and use it as a guide, so that you are ready when the director calls, "Action!"

Sample Page from Character Notebook

SCENE_____, PAGE_____

1. What happened to me when the last scene ended?
2. How did I feel at the end of the scene?
3. How much time in the story has passed since the last scene?
4. What major/minor events have happened to me since the last scene?
5. How do I feel at the beginning of this scene?
6. Where am I coming from right before this scene begins?
7. How do I feel about the other character in the scene?
8. In one sentence, what do I want from the other character?
9. What is the other character trying to get from me?
10. What are the actions that I choose to play to get what I want?
11. What happens in the scene? What do I do in the scene?
12. What is the primary conflict in the scene?
13. What are the obstacles and problems for me in the scene?
14. How are these obstacles and problems making things difficult for me?
15. Why is getting what I want important right now? What is the emotional reason that powers my objective?
16. What song or piece of music is my character's theme song?

Onset Notes

After you shoot a scene, it would be helpful to write down any notes about your performance, such as:

- Emotional state:
  - What was my emotional state at the end of the scene?
  - What happened? Was I humiliated? Did I cry? Did I celebrate some exciting news?
- Physical state:
  - Was I hungover? Exhausted from staying up all night?
- Physical actions:
  - Did I do any physicals actions in the wide shot that I will have to recreate in the medium or close-up shots? For example, "My character was nervous, so I kept twisting my wedding ring." Or "I removed pearls to symbolize emotionally suffocating or perhaps getting ready for battle," etc. Make sure in the scene that follows that this is the new starting look.
- Reaction from others:
  - How did the other character(s) react in the scene? Did they leave angry? Did they gently hug me? Did they gloat with satisfaction?
- Were there any line changes?
  - Cut reference to old boyfriend, introduced catch phrase, added line, etc.

Chapter Notes
- Movies and television are usually shot out of sequential order.
- Map out your character's circumstances, wants, and journey.
- Create a character notebook and answer the questions for each scene.
- Use your character notebook to review before you shoot each scene.
- Make notes in your character notebook after you shoot each scene.

PART TWO
THE ACTOR'S WORLD

8

ACTING FOR THE CAMERA

You have thoroughly prepared your character, and now it is time to get in front of the camera. When you step in front of the camera, things change. Acting for the camera requires technical skills that the actor must develop in order to succeed. For example, you can give an amazing performance, but, if you don't remain in the frame, it can't be used. The character is unaware of these technical requirements, but the actor must incorporate these skills into their performance.

The chapters in Part Two: The Actor's World are packed with techniques that can be mastered through repetition. These techniques will instantly improve your performance. The exercises in these chapters are focused on acting for a single camera. However, the principles of the exercises will transfer to working with multiple cameras. Each chapter focuses on a technical skill that you can master. These skills will assist the crew on set and the editor in post-production. They will allow the editor to create your best performance. But, as you practice these techniques, it's important to remember that technique alone will only get you so far. An exciting acting moment only works when it supports the technical demands for the camera. If you develop and combine the skills in the following chapters with your creative impulses, you will be on your way to becoming a professional actor on camera.

The Camera Is Your Tool

A carpenter uses a hammer to build a house, and you can use the camera to build your performance. How do you feel when the camera is looking at you? Does it make you feel nervous? Are you hoping to just "get through" the scene without making any mistakes? Acting teachers often say, "Just act natural and forget that the camera is even there." Their intentions are good, but this advice isn't always helpful. The problem is that you do know that the camera is there the entire time, watching your every move. No matter how much you try and forget about it, you can feel it peeking into your soul. So, why would you want to pretend it's not there? Why wouldn't you want it to see you? Many beginning actors tend to move their energy away from the camera when they are playing a scene, as if they want to hide from it, when their goal should be the exact opposite. I want to help you shift your perspective and build a positive relationship with the camera.

It is common to arrive on set excited for a day of shooting. Then, a few hours later, you become uncomfortable as that little eye of the lens stares at you. You sense that the camera is scrutinizing you, judging you. You try to focus and pretend that you aren't feeling these things, because you want to appear "professional." The more you try to convince yourself that it's not happening, the worse it becomes. If this sounds familiar to you, you can overcome it. I can assure you that you are not the only person who has let their nerves get the best of them when acting for the camera. What is it about the camera that makes us feel uncomfortable? How can we overcome this phenomenon? Often, we give too much power to this little machine that captures our image. There are many techniques to help you relax, and I encourage you to explore them all. However, I have found that the best place to start is by choosing your relationship to the camera and deciding to use it as a tool. The camera is not working against you. It's working with you. It's your friend. You need it, and you should be longing for it to see you.

Telling the Story Visually

Acting for the camera is a visual medium. You must be able to tell the story without words.

Exercise 8.1

Step One

Imagine a specific person in your mind.

Step Two

Pretend that you are seated on a park bench or on a sofa in a living room. Prepare the following three separate takes. See your imaginary person:

- Do something really funny … (e.g., dancing by themselves).
- Do something really tender … (e.g., feeding a sick animal).
- Experience something tragic … (e.g., sitting alone crying).

Step Three

See your imaginary person walk from one side of the camera to the other. Observe them performing the activity for 15–20 seconds for each take.

Step Four

Shoot all three scenes. Play back the footage and see if you are telling the story visually. Is your performance believable? Are you really seeing something specific? Are you forcing a reaction or are you experiencing what you are seeing in your imagination?

9

THE FRAME
PLAY THE PIECE OF PIE

The frame is your playing space. It is the picture that is seen through the viewfinder that has been framed by the cinematographer. Depending on the type of shot, you may have a lot of room to play or very little within the frame. The standard shots that involve actors are the master or wide, medium, medium close-up, close-up, extreme close-up, over-the-shoulder, and two shot. It is important that your movement matches from shot to shot so that it will be easy to edit together. So, as a general rule, keep your movement consistent for each shot.

To vary the visual storytelling, directors and cinematographers will utilize the above shots combined with a camera angle. There are four basic angles you may encounter.

1. *High angle* (*bird's-eye view or top shot*) is where the camera is positioned high (such as in a tree) and focused on the actor down below.
2. *Low angle* is where the camera is positioned low (such as in a car trunk) and looking up at the actor.
3. *Dutch tilt* is where the camera is tilted to one side to create a sense of unease or disorientation for the viewer.
4. *Point of view* (POV) is a first-person shot where the camera records the scene from a single character's viewpoint. It can also

Figure 9.1 Wide Shot. A wide shot (WS) is a large frame that is often used for the master shot. It is usually filmed first and covers all of the action from the beginning to the end of the scene. (Credit: John James Hickey)

Figure 9.2 Medium Shot. The medium shot (MS) is generally from the waist up. It gives the audience an opportunity to get closer to the character. (Credit: John James Hickey)

be used as a way to build tension, such as the climactic scene in *Silence of the Lambs* when Clarice Starling is searching for Buffalo Bill in his dungeon, and we see him stalking her through his night vision goggles.

Figure 9.3 Medium Close-Up Shot. The medium close-up shot (MCU) is from about the middle of the chest up. It is one of the most often used shots in acting for the camera, and it is the standard frame for self-tape auditions. (Credit: John James Hickey)

Figure 9.4 Close-Up Shot. The close-up (CU) is a tighter shot on the face. It frames the face from the top of the shoulders to the top of the head. It can capture more emotion than an MCU. (Credit: John James Hickey)

Figure 9.5 Extreme Close-Up Shot. The extreme close-up (ECU) is an even tighter shot focusing perhaps on just the eyes, lips, or gun trigger. (Credit: John James Hickey)

Figure 9.6 Over-The-Shoulder Shot. The over-the-shoulder shot (OTS) is when the camera is placed behind one actor's shoulder and focused on the other actor. The back of the first actor's shoulder and head is in the frame to help orient the viewer and establish a connection between the characters. (Credit: John James Hickey)

Figure 9.7 Two Shot. The two shot is when two actors are in the same frame. It is often used to show the emotional relationship between the two characters. There are many kinds of two shots. The most common is a 50–50 split, often used when two people are chatting at a café table. Another type of two shot is where the camera racks (shifts) focus back and forth from the background actor to the foreground actor. See in Figure 9.7 how the foreground character is the one that is in focus. (Credit: John James Hickey)

Where Is My Audience?

As an exercise, I will have two actors prepare a scene and sit across from each other. I will ask the on-camera actor, "Where is your audience?" Usually, the actor will point to the other actor and say, "They're my audience. I am speaking to them." You always want to connect to the other character, but your audience is the camera. The word *camera* is Italian for "room," and in that room are the sound and film editors looking to shape your performance. Remember, the camera is your friend, and you *want* it to see you. Always know where it is. Invite it into your world.

Play the Piece of Pie

Playing the Piece of Pie is a simple visual tool that will help improve your performance on camera. It is an imaginary triangle between you and both sides of the camera. The size of this imaginary pie changes when the frame changes. The bigger the frame, the larger the piece of pie. A wide shot is the size of half a pie, a medium shot is a quarter, and a close-up is a small slice. It isn't an exact science, but for most scenes you want to play within the imaginary pie when you look to the right or left of the camera. Directors will often tell you your framing. "Even though the camera is close, I have a wide-angle lens, so it will give you the freedom to capture your physical comedy." Or "We are using a zoom lens at a distance, but you are in a close-up." If the director or AD hasn't told you the frame, it's perfectly acceptable to ask. If they are busy, you can quickly ask the cinematographer or camera operator.

Sunset Boulevard

The 1950 film *Sunset Boulevard*[1] is a fantastic film about a silent-film star named Norma Desmond (played by Gloria Swanson) who dreams about making a triumphant return to the big screen. The film was nominated for 11 Academy Awards, including Ms. Swanson for Best Actress. She was an enormous star of the silent-film era, and in 1926 she became the fifth producing partner at United Artists[2]. Her performance in *Sunset Boulevard* is a wonderful example of an actor who uses the frame and plays within the imaginary piece of pie. Actors who were trained in the silent-film era had to develop this particular skill because they couldn't use dialogue. Watch her incredible performance in this movie and you will see how she plays her angles effectively. Early in the film, when William Holden's character recognizes her as an old silent-film star, he says to her, "I know your face. You're Norma Desmond. You used to be in silent pictures. You used to be big." She is in a medium frame and she pulls you right in when she says, "I am big. It's the pictures that got small." Notice how still she is and that, when she moves, it's within the piece of pie.

Use the scene below to practice playing the piece of pie in master, medium, and close-up shots. To help you with your angles, raise your hands up for each shot to create the borders of your imaginary triangle before you shoot the scene. Play the exact same actions, but adjust the size of the pie for each shot. For fun, do the opposite, watch the footage, and see how frustrating it is when you are not within the imaginary pie.

Scene 9.1

EXT. COUNTRYSIDE – DAY

CHARACTER A and CHARACTER B stand across from each other in the countryside. The camera is just to the left side of Character B, who is off camera. Character A looks to the right of the camera at the river. After a moment, Character A looks across the lens to the other side of the camera and at Character B.

CHARACTER A

I always loved coming here with you.

They smile at each other and Character A looks back to the river.

End of scene.

Exercise 9.1

Rehearse and shoot Scene 9.1 in wide, medium, and close-up shots while playing the piece of pie.

Wide

In this frame, your piece of pie is huge. Imagine an entire pizza pie and cut it right in half. You have a lot of room on each side of the camera to play.

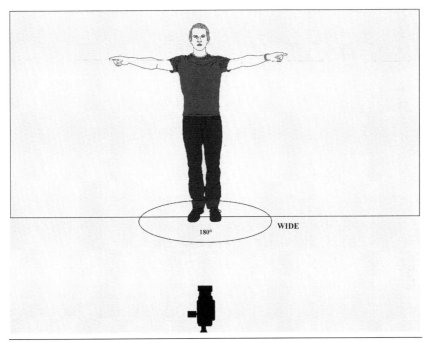

Figure 9.8 Piece of the Pie: Master Shot. (Credit: John James Hickey)

Medium

In this frame, your piece of pie is smaller than in the wide shot, but you still have a lot of playing space on each side of the camera.

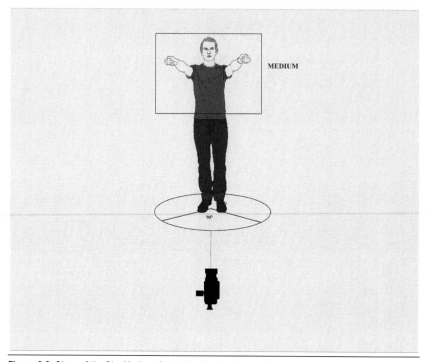

Figure 9.9 Piece of the Pie: Medium Shot. (Credit: John James Hickey)

Close-Up

In this frame, your piece of pie has become much tighter, with less room to move. The pie is now a small slice.

In time, playing the piece of pie will become second nature to you, and you won't even think about it. I have seen many actors develop this skill in a short amount of time. Practice playing your angles within the imaginary piece of pie until it becomes effortless. You can deliver an award-winning

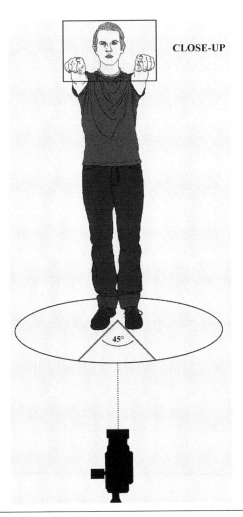

CLOSE-UP

Figure 9.10 Piece of the Pie: Close-up. (Credit: John James Hickey)

speech, but if we can only see the side of your face, you will probably wind up on the cutting room floor. Pull the audience into you and give the editor clear images to create the most dynamic scene. The editor will improve your performance, but only if you provide them with the images that they need.

Chapter Notes

- The camera is your audience.
- Keep your physical movements consistent from shot to shot so that they will match in editing.
- Play the piece of pie or imaginary triangle between you and both sides of the camera.
- The tighter the frame, the smaller the piece of pie.

10
SIZE
SCALING THE PERFORMANCE

Scaling Your Performance

The size of your performance is dictated by the character, frame, and style of the story. The distance between you and the camera is not important. What is important is the size of your frame. When the frame changes, the playing space changes. Scaling your performance on camera is similar to scaling the size of your acting on stage in a theatre. When you act in a theatre or on camera, you must be aware of the size of your playing space. Are you performing in a 1,200-seat theatre with an orchestra, mezzanine, and balcony? Or are you performing in a 25-seat coffee shop theatre in NYC's East Village? Are you performing in a wide shot? Or are you performing in a tight close-up?

Imagine taking the physical and vocal energy required to fill a 1,200-seat theatre and putting it into a 25-seat theatre with the audience only 10 feet away from you. It's hilarious when you think about it and could make for a great comedy. The audience would have to wear ear plugs and wipe the spit off their faces. You would literally blow them out of their seats. What if you acted in the 1,200-seat theatre as if you were in the 25-seat theatre? The audience wouldn't be able to hear or understand anything you do or say and, consequently, would demand their money back.

Figure 10.1 Blow them away with your performance, not with your volume. (Credit: John James Hickey)

Figure 10.2 In theatre you must play to the back of the house. In film, the "back of the house" is the microphone, which is at most only an arm's length away. (Credit: John James Hickey)

The Crew Is Not Your Audience

You will often hear film and television directors say that theatre actors are too big or theatrical for the camera. They will ask them to tone down their performance. This is common, because theatre actors, often subconsciously, think that they are performing for the crew on the set or the "live" audience watching the scene. As we've discussed, the camera is your audience. The crew could consist of 100 technicians or 3, and it should not affect your performance. Your performance should be scaled to the frame and style of the project, no matter how many people are on set. I'd like to point out that theatre actors can easily transition to acting for the camera if they desire. In fact, most actors that you watch on the screen were trained extensively in the theatre. If you are serious about acting, do theatre. It will teach you discipline and how to play a character. You will become an expert at performing night after night and making it appear as if it is happening for the first time. The skills that you learn from acting in the theatre are essential, but you must adjust them to the camera.

Work on Your Own Scale of 1–10

Think of your performance on your own scale of 1–10, where 10 would be the most energetic and largest size that you could play in the frame, and 1 would be the most subtle. You can apply this private scale to your physical movements, vocal energy, and intention that you are playing. Sometimes your actions may be wonderful choices, but you are just playing the wrong number on the scale. If a director tells you that you are being too big or too small, stay calm and change the number on your internal dial.

Acting in the Close-Up

You want to pull the audience into the frame with you, especially when you are acting in a close-up. The more you move, the less this will happen. You can express huge emotions on camera, but you must stay in the frame. Think about inviting the audience into your world and not reaching out to them. Legendary actor Marlon Brando once said, "In a close-up, the audience is only inches away, and your face becomes the stage."[1] The camera will read your thoughts. It will pick up any movement that you make. In a close-up, everything is magnified. You don't need to show or prove anything to the camera. Always remind yourself to breathe and clearly see any images that are in your mind as you listen to the other character. The close-up is the time for your most subtle acting. Be aware not to blink your eyes too much, especially in the close-up. The accomplished actor, Michael Caine, has discussed how blinking too much in the close-up can weaken your character[2]. Editors often spend hours attempting to edit around the moments where the actor is blinking on a key line. We all blink our eyes, and it is okay to blink a little on camera. However, be careful not to blink on your most important and emotional lines in a scene. Mark these moments in your script as you prepare. As an exercise, record yourself in a close-up saying the line "I love you" to a loved one. Try it once, blinking your eyes when you say the line. Then, try again with your eyes opened. Play it back, and I bet you will see a big difference. Identify the emotional lines in a scene and avoid blinking when you deliver them.

Sophie's Choice

Meryl Streep won the Academy Award for Best Actress for her brilliant performance in *Sophie's Choice*[3], where she plays a Polish Holocaust survivor in World War II. In a gut-wrenching scene at Auschwitz, a Nazi soldier forces Sophie to decide which of her two children will live and which one will die. In this haunting moment, she is filled with emotion and she begins to lose control as they yank her daughter away. She explodes with rage, but her movement is subtle. She stays in the frame of the close-up the entire time. The stillness of her physicality within the frame magnifies her emotional anguish. She knew the amount of room she had for the shot and she pulled the audience into her. When you are framed in a close-up shot, the camera will see exactly what you are thinking and feeling.

It Doesn't Always Have to Be Small

Be careful not to fall into the trap that all performances on camera are small, quiet, and subtle. If you watch some of the great performances in film and television, you will find this to be untrue. Watch Taraji P. Henson in her brilliant performance in the movie *Talk to Me*[4] with Don Cheadle. Her choices are fearless, exciting, and always believable. She uses her voice and body to activate the character within the frame and bring out some amazing acting moments. Is she acting too big for the frame? Not at all. She plays the character with precision and fills the frame. Then watch her performance in the Academy Award-nominated movie *Hidden Figures*[5] and you will see some incredibly subtle acting. She is outstanding in both roles. She plays the appropriate size for each frame, based on her character and the style of the film.

Sitcoms

You will find incredibly large and subtle comedic performances on American sitcoms. Watch classic sitcoms such as *Frazier*[6], *'black-ish*[7], and *How I Met Your Mother*[8]. Are these actors acting too big for the camera? Not in the least bit. Notice how these shows use wider frames that allow the actors to have more movement to bring out the comedic moments. Then, compare them with the subtle performances in the hilarious mockumentary-style television show *The Office*[9], starring Steve Carrell. The actors on these shows are incredible. The styles are very different. What makes them similar is that the actors play the style and scale the size of their performance to the frame.

Exercise 10.1

- Learn a dramatic or comedic monologue from one of your favorite films or television shows.
- Practice performing it in wide, medium close-up, and close-up shots.
- Play with your own scale of 1–10 with each shot.
- Experiment with monologues that are different styles.
- Watch your scene and make adjustments for each frame.

Chapter Notes

- The size of your performance is dictated by the character, frame, and style of the story.
- Act for the size of the frame, not the crew on set.
- Make adjustments with your own internal scale of 1–10.
- In a close-up, find stillness and keep your movements subtle.
- Avoid blinking on important or emotional lines.

11

ACTION
WHAT DO I DO NOW?

The director calls, "Action!" What should you do next? For many, the natural impulse is to quickly say your first line. But, if you wait a couple of moments (in character) before you say your first line, you will give the editor space to cut into the scene. You want to help them out by giving them a little room. If you fire away with your first line right after you hear "Action," the editor will be limited in the editing room. So, make the adjustment and allow for a little space. This small adjustment can make a world of difference for the post-production team.

Cutting on Movement

Editors often cut on a physical movement, because it's more interesting. This is an important concept for all of the lessons in this section. When you begin to understand how the editor works, your performance on camera will quickly improve. Watch your favorite movies and television shows with an editor's eye and you will see. Notice what the character is physically doing when the editor cuts to them. Now, sometimes an editor will cut on stillness between two characters to create tension or to emphasize an emotional moment. But often, they cut to a character who is reacting with a movement. Cutting on movement can help the scene not become flat. The same concept applies for cutting into the beginning of a scene on a physical action. Also, a little physical behavior can make the scene more believable. You should always connect the physical actions of your character to the given circumstances of the scene. They should never be random. This is simple to do, and it can make the scene much more dynamic. If you do develop this skill, you will provide the editor with many options. These physical actions can be large, such as grabbing a coffee cup, or they can be small, such as looking away from the other character with a subtle movement of your eyes. For example, in a particular scene, you could look down at the wedding invitations on the table and smile. After a moment, you could bring your focus up to your soon-to-be wife and deliver your first line, "I love you." Think of a way to create a specific physical action in the couple of beats between the director calling "Action" and your first line of dialogue. You want it to support and activate the scene. This small action will give the editor options when they cut into the beginning of the scene.

It's Like a Flipbook

When I was a young actor in New York City, I was fortunate to become friends with the producer, director, and Emmy Award-winning actor Timothy Busfield. Tim is such a giving artist and he quickly became a mentor. He continues to have an incredible career with iconic credits such as *For Life*[1], *Field of Dreams*[2], *Revenge of the Nerds*[3], *The West Wing*[4], and *Thirtysomething*[5]. I remember meeting him one night at an old restaurant on Broadway near Lincoln Center, and I asked him, "How do I become a better actor on camera?" I will never forget his advice. He told me, "In film acting, with a single camera, it's like an old flipbook. One image at a time tells the story." Think of your physical actions as a series of images that tell the story.

Connect and Breathe

The moment after you hear "Action!" is not a time to rush. It's a time for you to connect to the other character and situation. In addition to playing a small physical action, use these brief moments to feel yourself in the seat or your feet on the ground. Connect to your breath and invite the camera to look into you. Focus on the moment. Look inside the character across from you. Be curious about what they are feeling. Putting your attention on them will help you to relax. Breathe them in for a moment and lock in for the scene.

Exercise 11.1

Character A and B are siblings. They have recently found out that their grandmother has passed away. Imagine that you are playing Character A. Let's examine how giving the editor a little space can go a long way for them and you.

INT. – COFFEE SHOP – DAY

CHARACTER A and CHARACTER B sit in a coffee shop. Two espressos sit on the table. There is an uncomfortable silence.

CHARACTER A

I can't believe this is happening.

CHARACTER B

It's not the way I wanted things to be.

CHARACTER A

(beat)

Then why didn't you visit her more?

End of scene.

You are sitting in the chair across from Character B, waiting to start the scene, and suddenly the 1st AD calls the roll to begin the scene:

AD: Quiet on the set! Roll sound!
SOUND: Sound speeding.
AD: Roll camera.
CAMERA: Rolling.
AD: Mark it!

2ND AC: This is 12 Baker, Take #1. Mark. (claps the slate)
CAMERA: Frame set.
DIRECTOR: Settle everyone … Action!

You stare at Character B and you say your first line, "I can't believe this is happening."

Is this bad acting? No, but it will limit how the editor can cut the scene. Give them options by creating a simple action that supports the circumstances before you say your first line. Think about what fits the scene and the moment best. A small action or series of actions can make the scene more dynamic and give the editor more material to create with.

Physical Action Options

- You look at Character B and breathe them in for a moment.
- You give a simple smile to try and ease the tension.
- You look down at the espresso and think for a moment.
- You pick up the espresso and take a sip, and gently put it back down.
- You slowly look up at Character B and say, "I can't believe this is happening."

Now, you have given the editor multiple options and cutting points into the scene that support the story. When you give the simple smile, the editor could cut to Character B to see how they feel and create a moment of tension. When you pick up the espresso, the editor could cut to either character on that physical action. Or, the editor could choose to not use any of those physical actions and start from the moment after you put the espresso down when you are looking at Character B. With this specific movement, you have created tension and cutting possibilities for the editor. This is one of many options. Do you have to take a drink? No. Maybe that doesn't fit the moment. Perhaps you only put your hand on the cup and then look up to your sibling before you say your line. Or, maybe you just look at the espresso for a beat. Keep the actions specific, simple, and connected to the world of the character.

Chapter Notes

- When the director calls, "Action," allow two to three beats before the first line.
- Editors often cut on movement.
- Physical actions can be large or subtle.
- If it supports the scene, choose a simple physical action before your first line.
- Acting on camera is like a series of images in a flipbook.
- Use a couple of beats to connect to your breath, acting partner, and the situation.

12

THE ART OF THE REACTION
HELP THE EDITOR MAKE YOU LOOK GREAT

A reaction shot is when the editor cuts to a character's reaction to help tell the story. So much of acting for the camera is about listening and reaction shots. Before we dive into reaction shots, I want to be clear about something. I always want you to be in the moment and listening to your partner when you're acting on camera. I want you to act on your impulse and combine it with the technical skills that help the editor to create the performance. You can play an exciting scene and still not give the editor good footage to cut. Set them and you up for success by learning the art of the reaction.

Always Ask Why

Watch great film or television actors and pay close attention to when the editor cuts to a character for a reaction shot in a scene. Ask yourself, "Why did they cut there?" and "What did the character physically do in the reaction shot?" How did cutting at that specific moment help tell the story? Did the character look away? Look down? Take a breath? Could you tell what the character was thinking? Was the other character in the middle of a monologue when the editor cut for the reaction? Was the reaction shot during a shift in emotion between the two characters? If you want to improve your acting, watch your favorite performances and pay attention to the reaction shots.

Reaction Shot

Cutting for a reaction shot adds dimension and excitement to the scene. Any physical reaction you have should always be connected to the emotion of the moment. A reaction shot is usually a shift in focus connected to a feeling. It could be a breath of sadness as you slightly look away from the other character, your eyes disappointedly looking down in a close-up, or your character throwing their arms up in excitement after they've won a big game. Like a flipbook, the editor needs to be able to cut to a clear image to tell the story, and you must give it to them.

Scene 12.1 Reaction Shot

INT. CAFÉ – NIGHT

CHARACTER B is looking down reading a book.

CHARACTER A
You look great today.

Character B looks up and reacts with happiness.
Character B returns to reading a book.

CHARACTER A
Why would you wear that?

Character B looks up and reacts with sadness.

End of scene.

Exercise 12.1

- Shoot the scene in a medium close-up and close-up shot.
- Focus on not anticipating the moment by committing to reading the book.
- Slowly look up from the book and give the editor a clean reaction (flipbook).

Editors Are Magicians

Great editing is something that we often take for granted when watching a movie or television show, because we don't notice it. That means the editor is brilliant at their craft. Editors are magicians. They are the final screenwriter. The great ones will make your performance better than it was on set by cutting around your mistakes and stitching together your best takes. There is no exact science as to when an editor will cut for a reaction in a scene, but there are clues in the script that will help you give the editor the reactions they desperately want.

Cutting on Beats

Editors often cut for reaction moments where the *beat* is marked by the screenwriter. This isn't because the editor sees the word *beat* in the script and then cuts for a reaction as part of a formula. It's because the *beat* provides a natural transition or emotional shift between the characters in the scene.

What does the word *beat* in your script mean? Why did the screenwriter put it there? Is it meant to be a pause? If so, how long? What is happening during that pause? *The beat that is marked in your script by the screenwriter is an indication of a change in thought or shift in emotion between the characters.* Often, it's when a character makes a discovery or has an epiphany. This is an excellent spot to have a reaction because it shows how your character feels about the change that is occurring. The editor may or may not use your reaction during the beat, but give them the option.

Cutting on Eye Movement

Editors often cut on the eye movement when one character looks to another. We see this a lot in multiple character scenes when one character looks to the other character before they speak. Cutting on your eye movement as you look to the other character provides logic for the scene. Think about how you can look to another character to set up their next line. How can you help the editor out by giving them a logical reason to cut on action? Also, for example, when a character sets an important prop on a table, follow it with your eyes. This will give the editor an opportunity to cut to the prop if it serves the story.

Scene 12.2

You are playing Character A. *The camera is focused on you and placed between the two off-camera detectives.*

EXT. PARK – DAY

Character A is walking in the park. Detective #1 and Detective #2 quickly approach. They stop.

CHARACTER A
Are you going to keep following me?

DETECTIVE #1 (O.S.)
We just wanted to ask you a couple of questions.

DETECTIVE #2 (O.S.)
An innocent child lost their life.

CHARACTER A
I told you everything.

End of scene.

You know that Detective #1 has the second line in the scene. So, which detective do you look at when you deliver your first line – Detective #1 or #2? Many actors would deliver their first line to Detective #1 because they have the next line, but this choice gives the editor fewer ways to cut the scene. Give them the option to cut on your eye movement to set up the next line in the scene.

Because you know that Detective #1 will answer your question, then maybe deliver your first line to Detective #2. This way, when Detective #1 begins to answer your question, you can look across the camera to them. Now, the editor can cut on your movement. Then, when Detective #2 says, "An innocent child lost their life," you can look back across the camera to Detective #2. This will give the editor another opportunity to cut on your movement.

Exercise 12.2

- Record yourself playing the scene three different ways in a medium close-up shot:
  - First, play the scene delivering your first line to Detective #1.
  - Second, play the scene delivering your first line to Detective #2. Allow Detective #1's line, "We just wanted to ask you a couple of questions," to pull your focus across the camera to them.
  - Third, begin the scene looking at Detective #1. Have your eyes cross the camera and deliver your first line, "Are you going to keep following me?" to Detective #2 (cutting point 1). Allow Detective #1's line, "We just wanted to ask you a couple of questions," to pull your focus across the camera back to them (cutting point #2). Allow Detective #2's line, "An innocent child lost their life," to pull your focus across the camera back to them (cutting point #3), and deliver your last line to Detective #2.
- Play back the footage and observe the cutting points on your eye movement.

There isn't one correct way to play the scene. Think about the cutting points and make choices.

Cutting on Emotional Words

What does the other character say that affects you emotionally in the scene? What information do you receive that sparks a thought, idea, or emotional response? When you hear these emotional words, what does it stir in you? These emotional words are golden opportunities for you to give a clear reaction. Study the other character's lines, circle the emotional words for your character, and imagine how this could create a reaction.

Cutting on Monologues

When a character has a speech or monologue, the editor wants to cut to the character who is listening to break up the monologue. Usually, it's boring to keep the camera on the character speaking for a long period of time. If you are playing the character that is listening to a monologue, know that the editor wants to cut to you. If they cut to you more than once, this is a sign that you are doing some great acting. It means that you are giving them reactions that they feel compelled to use. If the editor never cuts to you listening to the other character's monologue, this is usually bad news. This is probably an indication that you didn't give the editor any reason to cut to you because you were just staring blankly at the other character for the entire speech. Editors will search through the footage looking for a chance to cut to you. They will get frustrated if you aren't giving them any reaction to help tell the story. Your job is to give them options, and their job is to decide how to put it together. Professor Perlman's heartwarming speech to his son Elio in the Academy Award winning film *Call Me by Your Name*[1] is a fine example of how editor Walter Fasano masterfully held our attention during Perlman's long monologue toward the end of the film. The scene, exquisitely played Michael Stuhlbarg (Professor Perlman) and Timothée Chalamet (Elio), starts in a two shot. Then, halfway through the monologue, Fasano holds the shot on the father and cuts to Elio's reaction three times, which gives us three snapshots (flipbook) of Elio's emotional state. Director Luca Guadagnino and Fasano provide us with another remarkable reaction shot. It is an epic 4-minute close-up of Elio during the end credits. As Sufjan Stevens's "Visions of Gideon"[2] gently plays in the background, Elio, heartbroken, stares into the fire and takes us on a compelling, nuanced emotional journey. It's masterful. Acting on camera requires you to always have an inner life for your character. You must have a clear inner monologue expressing your thoughts and feelings when you don't have words.

Whenever you play someone who is listening to a character deliver a long speech, study that character's monologue and circle the key emotional words in the speech. Do those words cause you to have an emotional response and a physical shift? The answer is probably "yes," and the editor will be happy if you can deliver reactions in those key moments.

Cross-Camera Reaction

A cross-camera reaction is when you cross the lens with your eyes to the other side of the camera. When used effectively, it is a powerful storytelling tool.

Going cross-camera allows you to work both sides of the camera to add nuance. If all of your reactions move away from the camera, we will see the side of your face more than we will see your eyes. Most actors are nervous to look across the camera because they are afraid that they may "spike the lens" (look directly into it). Remember, you want to use the camera to your advantage. Be brave, but be selective. When you go cross-camera, move smoothly as you cross the lens. If you accidentally look into the lens for a second, keep going and never stop the scene. The director is in charge of when to cut a scene. Your job is to play the character as believably as you can.

A wonderful spot to go cross-camera for a reaction is on the most pivotal and emotional transitions in the scene. These transitional moments are usually toward the end of the scene, when your character receives information that may change their point of view. Practice your cross-camera reaction, play the piece of pie, and have fun working both sides of the camera.

Scene 12.3

Character B has just been accepted to a prestigious and expensive music conservatory, but their family doesn't have the money to send them.

CHARACTER B

This is my dream. Why don't you care about me?

CHARACTER A

I don't care about you? Do you think it's been easy raising you by myself? I have worked two jobs for ten years, so that you could take classes. We just don't have the money.

(*beat*)

I'm sorry. I love you.

End of scene.

Analysis

Beat Reaction

When Character A says, "money," this is a moment of disappointment for Character B. If you are playing Character B, how will you react to this emotional word? How does it make you feel? Do you physically shift? If it's in a close-up, maybe you take a breath as your eyes shift downward. Then, when Character A says, "I love you," you could receive this heartfelt line and slowly look back to them.

Emotional Words

There are many emotional words where you could react. Study the monologue. Make your own choices. Think about the words that affect your character the most, such as *worked two jobs*, *take classes*, *money*, and *love you*. These are all great opportunities for a reaction shot.

Exercise 12.3

- Record the scene in a medium close-up.
- Have an acting partner play Character A's monologue off-camera.
- Play Character B listening to the monologue.
- Circle the beat and the most powerful emotional words.
- Practice reacting to the emotional words and during the beat.
- Listen to Character A and be selective.
- Play back and watch the footage. Are your reactions clear?

Chapter Notes

- A reaction shot is when the editor cuts to a character's reaction to help tell the story.
- When an editor cuts to a reaction, ask "Why?" What does the character physically do in the reaction?
- Cutting for a reaction adds dimension to the scene.
- A good place to have a reaction is during the beat and on key emotional words.

- In a multiple-character scene, give the editor an opportunity to cut on your eye movement.
- Give the editor reactions on key words when your character is listening to a monologue.
- Always have an inner monologue when you aren't speaking.

13

HITTING THE MARK
SKILL VERSUS TALENT

The Mark

The mark is where the director positions you for a scene. Marks are usually identified with a T-shaped piece of spike tape on the ground. It is important that you land directly on it. Arriving on your mark at the intended moment is known as "hitting your mark." When there are scenes with multiple characters, each character will have their own colored spike tape. Every time a character moves, a new mark is placed where they must land. Sometimes, depending on your blocking, you have multiple marks in a scene. When the director wants to shoot another "take" from the top of the scene, you will be instructed to go *back to one* or back to your first position. An actor consistently hitting their mark is a sign of a professional. Hitting your mark doesn't require talent, but it is an essential skill that must be developed if you want to work in the profession.

Why Is the Mark Important?

Sometimes, on sets, you will hear the complaint, "The actor is missing their mark." When you miss your mark, you affect the focus and the picture in the frame. If it is an over-the-shoulder shot, you may block the camera from filming the on-screen actor. Missing your mark wastes valuable time and costs the entire production money. Production schedules

Figure 13.1 Spike Marks. (Credit: John James Hickey)

are tight, and they operate on challenging budgets. Therefore, being efficient is vital to the overall success of the project. Recently, a student of mine had a bit part on a feature film. When I asked her how it went, she said, "Pretty good, but the lead actor couldn't hit their mark take after take." Apparently, the director and the entire crew quickly became frustrated, and the actor became flustered. I have sympathy for this actor, but I was happy that my student learned such a valuable lesson that day.

Cinematographers

Cinematographers design each shot like a painting. The placement of the camera, lights, and where you are positioned are all given a lot of thought. These elements bring the scene to life. When you miss your mark, it alters the shot and vision of the story. Imagine nailing your performance in a scene. Then, you find out that the cinematographer accidentally moved the camera during the shot, or the focus puller wasn't paying attention. This would be frustrating. You may think, "How dare they mess up my brilliant acting moment?" Well, that's how they feel when you miss your mark. Cinematographers will do everything that they can to help you to save the shot, but you must help them, too. After all, you're working together toward the same goal. The brilliant cinematographer Piero Basso, AIC (*Una Famiglia* – Venice International Film Festival, *Dafne* – Berlin International Film Festival, *Seven Acts of*

Mercy – Locarno International Film Festival) said this about the actor hitting their mark:

> As a cinematographer, I want the actor to feel free to act, and I do everything I can do to capture truthfully their performance. At the same time, if the actor misses the marks it affects the frame and focus sometimes beyond repair. While the focus can be corrected and adjusted by a good focus puller, although a challenging and complex process, the framing issues often result in the necessity of repeating the take because, in most cases, the frame is precisely lined up to offer a composition that reflects the vision of the director. Any changes invalidate the intention of the creative team.
>
> While designing a shot, I work with the actor to identify potential issues to hit the mark at the right time in relationship to my camera and the lighting. I always try to account in my lighting, framing, and focus a certain margin of error to allow the actor to concentrate on the performance. A veteran actor with advanced skills can land on their mark while staying emotionally connected in the scene, and that's the goal.

The Focal Plane

The focus on a camera operates on a horizontal plane. This means that you will remain in focus if you move to your left or right. However, the focus will be affected if you suddenly move closer toward the camera or back away from it. You will cross the focal plane and not be in focus. The tighter your frame, the more precise you must be. For example, if you miss your mark in a close-up, you will quickly become out of focus and pop out the frame. This creates unusable footage. The crew will have to reset and shoot the scene again. A common mistake that inexperienced actors make is that they move too much in the shot. I particularly see this when actors are seated in a chair. There is no need to lean forward and back on every other line to express how you feel. Allow the camera to come to you. Only move when you have a reason.

The Titanic Actor

A Titanic actor is an actor who constantly shifts their weight back and forth when standing on their mark. On a boat, you are constantly swaying because of the movement of the water. It can be unsettling. If you continuously shift your weight with large movements, you may sway in and out of the frame. This can be distracting and potentially problematic for the editor. The tighter the shot (close-up), the less room you have to shift your weight. If the editor wants to cut the scene using different takes, it may appear that you are bouncing back and forth with each cut. Also, this can be an issue if you frequently shift your weight from one side to the other when you are seated in a chair. So, anchor down on your mark. However, you shouldn't be frozen or locked, either. Your character should have natural movements, but avoid large, unnecessary weight shifts that alter the frame.

How to Hit Your Mark

As soon as you have been given your mark, immediately begin to practice how you are going to get there. You want to rehearse moving from your starting point to your mark so that you are comfortable before the director calls "Action." You may only have a minute before the crew is ready to shoot. Quickly use this time to get comfortable with the movement. It will relax you before the camera rolls.

Visual Marks

When you are standing on your mark, look for other visual reference points in the space that will help you get to your mark. For example, if you are shooting a scene in a living room, you may notice that if you are in alignment with the chair to the left, you will be on your mark. Perhaps you can land directly on your mark by using a shadow line created by the lights if you are shooting on a sound stage. Look for anything that you can easily see in your soft focus that will help you get to the spot where you need to land. Take in the entire space and look for visual reference points.

Look Directly at the Mark

Another way to hit your mark is to look directly at it as you stand on it. This can make the scene more dramatic, and it gives the editor additional cutting points when you look back up from the mark to the other character. For any scene where you have to hit the mark, ask yourself, "Can I have my character look at the mark to help tell the story?" This can make your performance look more natural and interesting. However, you must always justify why your character would be looking down at the mark.

Example

Let's imagine that you are playing a young parent and your 10-year-old child has just cheated on a test at school. In the scene, your child is standing in the kitchen. When the principal from school called you earlier with the news, you began to rack your brain and ask yourself, "Where did I go wrong?" You quietly walk into the kitchen from the other room. You stop for a moment and look at your child standing there in shame. You walk across the room and look directly at the mark on the floor. You have your head slightly down because it hurts too much to look them in the eye. Finally, you land on your mark. You wait a moment, not knowing what to say. Then, you slowly look up at them and deliver your line. This way, you bring the conflict into the scene and you justify why your character is looking down. By incorporating this little technique, you have successfully blended the *character's world* and the *actor's world* together. It adds life to the scene, and it gives the editor more options to cut on movement because you have provided a physical action before you say your line.

Scene 13.1 INT. HOSPITAL ROOM – DAY

The patient lies in bed, and the Emergency Room Doctor enters.

DOCTOR
Good news. The results were negative, but we're going to have to take a couple more tests before we can be sure.

End of scene.

Exercise 13.1

- Learn the sample scene above and practice hitting your mark with both techniques.
- Give yourself a mark on the floor by placing piece of tape in the shape of a "T" on the floor.
- Challenge yourself by having about 10 feet between your first position and your mark.
- Land on your mark before you deliver your line.
- Try using a prop such as a folder in your hands to justify looking down at the mark as you land on it.

Chapter Notes

- Your mark is the piece of tape on the floor indicating where you stand.
- If you miss your mark, it alters the frame and focus of the shot.
- Avoid large weight shifts back and forth throughout the scene.
- Techniques to hit your mark: visual marks; look at the mark.

14

PHYSICAL CONTINUITY
ACTING WITH PROPS

Physical continuity is repeating the same physical actions for each take of the scene. This will help the editor cut smoothly from shot to shot. It's especially important when your character uses props in a scene. Physical continuity will never be perfect, and that's okay. If you watch closely, you will often find physical continuity mistakes in movies and television shows. However, if you master physical continuity, you will help the editor create the best scene possible.

Spontaneous versus Technical

The best acting is spontaneous *within* the structure of the scene. Some people believe that acting is either spontaneous or technical, but it can be both. You can be consistent with your physical continuity and be spontaneous within the structure. Acting should be rehearsed so that it is repeatable but gives the illusion that it is happening for the first time. Depending on the shot list, you may have to shoot ten takes of a scene. So, consistency is key. Form provides freedom. Physical continuity is similar to the first time that you rehearse your blocking. It feels strange because you haven't practiced it. But, by the third rehearsal, it becomes natural and effortless. It is not about being exact, but it is about giving the editor every chance to make your performance shine. And, if you are consistent, editors will silently thank you when they are in post-production. Editor

Sean Robinson (ViacomCBS, Manhattan Film Festival, Long Island International Film Expo) had this to say about physical continuity:

> It is extremely challenging to edit a scene with an actor who has no control over their physical and temporal continuity. Editors look for cutting points based on movement. The movements should be consistent for every angle. Otherwise, it's a nightmare for the editor and increases the post-production budget because more hours are spent fixing actor problems.

Preparation

Practice your physical continuity before you arrive on the set but be willing to adjust if the director has a different idea. Directors want you to come in with choices, but they also want you to be flexible to new direction. Study the script closely, and you will get an idea of what props will most likely be used. For example, if your character is having a lunch on a beautiful terrace, you can assume that there will be silverware and glasses. How could you use any of these props to help tell the story?

Treat your physical continuity like blocking. Map it out at home when you are rehearsing. Mark your script with little crosses on the right-hand side of the page where your character uses a prop. If the director has a different vision, adjust. Making adjustments is one of the most important skills that you can develop as an actor. Don't let your ego get in the way. Every artist involved on a production prepares before they arrive on set. The director is in pre-production preparing for weeks or months. The wardrobe and make-up crews run tests to ensure all the characters have the right look. A storyboard artist draws out the shots to create a visual map. Everyone prepares, and you should, too.

Keep It Simple

You don't want to overcomplicate things with so many physical actions that you can't keep track of them. Less is more when it comes to physical continuity. Analyze your script and look for ways to use your props to help tell the story in the most interesting way. It wouldn't be wise to take a sip of your drink five times in a scene for no apparent reason other than to look "natural." This will be difficult for you to track and probably distracting for the viewer. Conversely, it may not look natural either if you don't touch anything for 3 minutes. Ask yourself, "When and why does my character use the prop?" Another important question to ask yourself is, "Is there a way that using the prop will activate the story and my character's objective?" Find ways to connect the physical continuity to the motivations of your character.

On the Beat

A good place to use a prop in a scene is on beat or topic transitions. This allows the scene to feel more natural because there is a shift in emotion or subject change between the characters. The major transition at the end of a scene is a wonderful opportunity to use your prop. Find the place near the end of the scene where the major transition occurs. Think about using a prop during that transition and connect it to your character's point of view. If you look for it, you will notice professional actors doing this in your favorite films and television programs.

Use Your Props Like A Pro

Christina Hendricks uses props like a pro. She played Joan Holloway on the hit television show *Mad Men*[1]. There is a wonderful scene in Season 4 where she is having a conversation with Roger Sterling (John Slattery) in a restaurant. She is sitting in a restaurant with a cigarette in her right hand held up in the air above her right shoulder. It's an amazing image of a confident character listening as Roger Sterling tries to win her love. The smoke hovers above her head, and she only takes one drag of the cigarette during the entire scene. In the final moment, she looks at Sterling and says her last line. She puts the cigarette out in the ashtray, grabs her fork, takes a bite of cheesecake, and looks back at him. This is brilliant acting. She keeps the physical continuity simple by taking only one drag from the cigarette. She creates a strong ending moment by extinguishing the cigarette in the ashtray and taking a bite of the cheesecake. Her physical actions support her character's action of pushing him away, and she gave the editor multiple cutting points (physical action) for the scene.

Scene 14.1

EXT. CAFÉ – DAY

Character A and B sit at a small café table.

CHARACTER A

So, how was the date?

CHARACTER B

Good.

CHARACTER A

Come on. Tell me.

CHARACTER B

It was … interesting.

CHARACTER A

Are you going to see him/her/them again?

CHARACTER B

Perhaps …
> (beat)

… you'll have to wait and see.

End of scene.

Exercise 14.1

- Prepare Character A or B with a partner.
- Select a prop that is appropriate for your character to use (smartphone, coffee cup, eyeglasses, lipstick, book, etc.).
- Choose two places to use your prop and mark them with a cross in your script.
- Challenge yourself to use the prop to propel the story.
- Use the prop where the beat is marked for one of your physical actions.
- Shoot the scene in wide, over-the-shoulder, and close-up shots.
- Play them back and see if you matched the physical continuity.
- Shoot both characters and try to edit the scene together. Notice if there are any limitations because of the physical continuity.

Chapter Notes

- Physical continuity is repeating the same physical actions for each take of the scene so that the editor can cut smoothly.
- Practice your physical actions until they feel natural.
- Mark your physical continuity on your script with little crosses.
- Keep your physical continuity simple so that you can repeat it, and it won't be distracting.
- Use your prop to activate the story.

15
VOICE
PLAY THE DISTANCE

Vocal Energy

Should you have a well-trained voice for film and television? Yes. But isn't that only for theatre actors? No. Shouldn't acting on camera always be quieter because of the microphones? Not necessarily. Acting for the camera requires you to have a strong vocal instrument more often than you may think. You will become a more versatile actor if you have a voice that is flexible and expressive. The power for your voice comes from air that you exhale. Vocal training helps strengthen your diaphragm and teaches you how to control your breath as it goes through the vocal folds and resonates throughout your body. Your voice is a muscle and it needs to be developed to express emotional range. Your voice requires proper exercise and protection from overuse. Find a good vocal or singing coach who will nurture your voice. You want to work with a caring teacher who will help you build a healthy vocal instrument. Vocal coaches are not only for singers. They're for actors, and they will help you improve your performance on camera. Once you begin working with a coach, have them help you develop a 10-minute vocal warm-up that you can do on set. You want to be connected to your breath and have your vocal engine ready to go before you step in front of the camera. Your lips and tongue should feel loose so that you don't trip over your words in the middle of the scene. Warming up your voice shouldn't be overlooked. Remember, once the camera begins to roll, there is no turning back.

Play the Distance

Always play the vocal distance between you and the other character. See your words land on your partner and make sure that they receive the message that you are sending. The distance between you and your partner may be 2 or 20 feet. Either way, use the vocal energy needed to reach the other character. When I first moved to New York City, a fellow actor friend got his first TV gig. He was an incredible actor in the theatre, but he had never performed on camera. He was excited for the opportunity. This was going to be his first television job. After he shot the episode, I asked him, "How did it go?" "Terrible," he replied. He told me that he thought he had to be quiet because of all the microphones. When the camera rolled, he began to almost whisper his lines. At the end of the scene, the director called, "Cut" and told him, "Hey, we can't hear you. Speak up!" Suddenly, he began to feel self-conscious and, on the next take, he blurted out his lines to make up for the previous one. Again, the director called, "Cut!" He added, "Let's do it again, and this time, just talk to her." Now he became more nervous. He could feel the tension in the room, and he knew that he was slowing down the production. On the third take, he was able to deliver what the director needed. Finally, they moved on to the next scene. In the end, he survived, but he learned a valuable lesson that day: *play the distance.* He has continued to have a successful career in film and television.

Microphones

Let the sound crew do their job. Don't worry about speaking to the boom microphone above your head or the body microphone tucked away under your shirt. Your vocal performance will be good if you focus on communicating your thoughts, feelings, and actions to the other character in the scene. For example, if you are having an intimate conversation in a quiet church, 2 feet away from the other character, play that distance and maintain the intimacy of the moment. If the sound crew needs you to be a little louder, they will tell you.

Not All Scenes Are Quiet

The 1993 movie *Philadelphia*[1] was one of the first mainstream motion pictures to address homosexuality, homophobia, and the AIDS crisis. It stars Tom Hanks, Denzel Washington, and many other outstanding actors. It is an emotionally packed story with incredible performances. In the film, Denzel Washington plays Joe Miller, the lawyer representing Andy Beckett (Tom Hanks), who was fired by his law firm for being gay and diagnosed with AIDS. Mr. Washington gives a beautiful perform-ance throughout the entire film. Pay close attention to the scenes where Miller speaks to the courtroom. As he addresses the court, he fluctuates his voice, using different vocal levels and pitches to reach each person in the room. It's a wonderful example of an accomplished theatre and screen actor using his well-trained voice with the same skill as a concert violinist.

Overlapping Dialogue

The production team prefers to have all character dialogue "clean" when there is only one person's mouth in the frame. If you speak your line on top of another actor's line, they will be recorded together. This will limit what the editor can do. Editor Sean Robinson (ViacomCBS, Manhattan Film Festival, Long Island International Film Expo) said, "Many times actors rush through their words or actions, and it's a nightmare in post. Editors spend hours and hours fussing with a word that is cut off by another actor trampling on their line." If you are shooting a wide master or a two shot, it won't be an issue because the camera will see both actor's mouths in the shot. However, if you are in a close-up or an over-the-shoulder shot, the sound recordist will want to have a "clean" take of your dialogue. This will allow the editor more options in post-production. So, allow a little space between your and the other actor's lines when you are in an over-the-shoulder, medium close-up, or close-up shot.

Monologue 15.1

CHARACTER A

Can I talk to you? Hey, can I talk to you? I have something that I need to say. I want you to apologize for everything that you did.

> (beat)

You know, I thought you were different, but I guess you're not.

End of scene.

Exercise 15.1

- Learn and prepare Monologue 15.1.
- Use your imagination and create your own given circumstances, relationship, objective, obstacles, and actions.
- Record yourself on camera playing it 2 feet away from the other character (intimate voice), 6 feet away (medium voice), and then 20 feet away (big voice).
- Play the distance and send your voice to the other character.

Chapter Notes

- Get a vocal coach and start training to improve your instrument.
- Play the distance between you and the other character.
- Let the sound technicians do their job and don't worry about the microphone.
- Always warm up before you appear on camera.

16

CAMERA TIME

WORK WITH THE CAMERA

When you're acting on camera, sometimes things move a little slower than they do in real life. They move in *camera time*. In camera time, you feel the camera and bring it along with you to ensure that your actions are captured in the frame. You are always working *with* the camera operator. You form a team that is creating the scene together. Be aware of your tempo when you are working with the camera operator. Pretend that there is an imaginary elastic band between you and the camera at all times. In general, the tighter the frame, the slower you move. Remember, the camera needs to see each image to tell the story. Of course, this doesn't mean that you move mechanically or too slowly. You should move fluidly, without rushing, and with the camera operator.

Sitting and Standing

Many scenes will require you to sit or stand during the scene. This is an area where beginning actors often make things difficult for the camera operator. If you move too fast, they will have trouble keeping you in the frame. If you move too slow, they will be waiting for you. Move at a pace that allows the camera operator to move with you so that you are working with and not against them. When you sit down or stand up, slightly cheat your eye-line up so that the camera is not focused on the top of your head. This will allow the camera to catch a little more of your face. It's a subtle adjustment, but it makes a difference.

Scene 16.1

INT. OFFICE – DAY

Character A enters their office and sits at the desk. The phone rings and they answer it.

> CHARACTER A
> Good afternoon. How can I help you? Yes, that's my child. Yes
> … uh huh …
> (listens with growing concern)
> I'll be right there.

Character A hangs up the phone, grabs their belongings, and quickly leaves.

End of scene.

Exercise 16.1

You are playing Character A. Take your time sitting down in the chair and bring the camera with you. Move naturally, but in camera time. Work with the camera operator to keep you in the frame. When you receive the phone call with urgent news about your child, don't jump out of the seat so quick that you bounce out of the frame. Play a sense of urgency, let the moment land, and take care of the camera as you get up out of the chair. We must see the image of you in a panic to know how your character feels.

- Get a partner and shoot the scene with a handheld camera.
- Practice working with the camera operator.
- Try to bring the camera with you when you sit down and when you get up to exit.
- See if you can play the emotional stakes of the scene while staying in the frame.

Close-Up … Slow Down

What about acting in the close-up with only your hand or foot? This is called an *insert* or a *cutaway* and is not as simple as it may sound. Practicing now will help you deliver on a real set. The last thing that you want is to hold up a production crew because you're the actor that can't move their hand and keep it in frame at the same time. These insert shots are key to the success of the story, and you need to be able to execute them.

Scene 16.2

Imagine that you are playing a character who is waiting for their romantic partner in an outdoor plaza. There are tourists moving about as you wait. Over the last few months, the two of you have grown apart. You have decided to end the relationship. As you wait, you begin to daydream about the good times you've had together. Subconsciously, you bring your hand up to your heart. The camera moves to a close-up on your hand and we see the ring on your finger. You've been directed to slowly bring your hand down toward your waist as the camera focuses on you twirling the ring with your thumb.

Exercise 16.2

Shoot the scene with a partner and stay in the world of the character. Slowly, move your hand up to your heart and down to your waist while keeping it in the frame. Can you bring the camera with you and stay in the frame? Switch roles with your partner and try operating the camera. This is a great way to learn how frustrating it can be if the actor moves too quickly.

- Find a spot to shoot the scene.
- Practice living in the character's given circumstances while executing the blocking for your hand in the close-up.
- Practice until you get comfortable balancing both worlds.

Walk and Talk

A *walk and talk* is exactly what it sounds like. It's a scene when you are walking and talking with one or more characters. They are common on political or police shows, but they are also used on many others. They are fun to play, but they do present a few challenges. The camera will be in front of you. The camera operator and crew will be slowly moving backwards, as you walk forward and play the scene. Two things you want to focus on are *blocking* and *pace*.

You want to find a rhythm with your scene partner and do your best to have your dialogue delivered at the same geographical points. This will help the editor if they want to cut to a different camera angle during the scene. If you are in the same location for each bit of dialogue, the edit will be easy to match. You want your pace to be a little slower and even paced so that the camera operator will be able to keep you in the frame. If you move too fast, they may have trouble keeping you in focus. So, slow down a little and move in camera time. Find an even pace and work *with* the camera team.

Scene 16.3

Character A and B are walking along a canal.

CHARACTER A

So, this is where you grew up?

CHARACTER B

Yeah. It's been a while since I have been here. It's … hard.

CHARACTER A

I know.

CHARACTER B

More difficult than I imagined.

CHARACTER A

(beat)

I'm sorry about your dad. I wish that I could have met him.

CHARACTER B

You would've liked him. He was so funny.

They stop for a moment.

                    CHARACTER B
     Can I show you something?
                    CHARACTER A
     Sure.

They smile at each other.

                    CHARACTER B
     I think you'll like this.

They exit to the left of the camera.

End of scene.

Exercise 16.3

- Get a partner and learn either Character A or Character B.
- Play the scene as a walk and talk.
- Create blocking and practice saying your lines at the same points.
- See if you can slow down a little and find a smooth rhythm.
- Have another friend shoot the scene with a handheld camera.

Chapter Notes

- Camera Time moves a little slower than real life.
- Move with the camera.
- Move slower in a tight frame.
- When you sit or stand bring the camera with you.
- Cheat your eye-line up a little so the camera gets a little more of your face.
- Keep your blocking consistent with the dialogue and have a steady pace.

17

THE FINAL BEAT

FOCAL SHIFTS AND CUTTING POINTS

The best camera actors give the editor multiple cutting points at the end of the scene. Watch any of your favorite films or television shows and pay close attention to what actors do in the final moments of a scene. What should you do after the last line has landed? One thing you shouldn't do is freeze like a statue. Keep acting after the last beat has landed and don't wait for the director to call cut. This will limit the editor's choices in cutting the ending of the scene. You want to create additional moments of behavior after the last line has landed and give the editor an opportunity to cut on your movement. American film and theatre director Paul Warner directed the movie *Fall Time*[1], starring Mickey Rourke and Stephen Baldwin, which premiered at the Sundance Film Festival. He had this to say about acting in the final moment of a scene:

> The final beat of a scene is, perhaps, the most critical in that this is the moment when one's character has a reaction to the climatic action of the scene. In other words, the cathartic beat in which the impulses erupt organically in relation to a dramatic realization. This moment is key in that it triggers the editorial transition into the next scene. It is one in which the character transforms and may decide to take action in pursuit of their

objective. Technically, there needs to be some kind of focal point and breath shift ... or a physical shift that illuminates an internal transformation. This is why a good director would never cut at the end of a scene until the actor's spontaneous impulses erupt.

Physical actions and shifts in focus will provide the editor with options to cut the final beat. It will allow them to visually tell the story and make the scene more dynamic.

Hold the Final Beat – Focal Shift

The end of a scene is a powerful storytelling moment. You want to give the editor a clear image in the final beat of the scene before you physically move. Avoid rushing and cluttering it up with sporadic movement. After you deliver or receive the last line in a scene, hold it for a moment before you move. Don't freeze, but let it linger for a second. As a reminder, you must be emotionally connected to what your character is thinking and feeling. For example, if you give the editor a clean moment after the last line that holds for 2 seconds, they can cut it down to 1.5 seconds, 1.2 seconds, or 0.8 seconds. Based on the scene, this moment could be shared with another character or be you by yourself. If it is shared with another character, focus on them and hold the moment for a couple of beats before you move. If your character is alone, sit in the moment for a couple of beats before you move. After you hold the final beat for a moment at the end of the scene, shift your focus to give the editor an ending cutting point. Depending on the story, this could be shifting your gaze to either side of the camera or downward and back to your original focal point. If you move too soon, it will be messy, and the editor will be challenged. Remember, you want the movement to be spontaneous and connected to the emotional life of your character. Give the editor a strong moment, and they will create a strong ending.

Here are examples of how you can play the final beat and give the editor three places to cut the end of the scene. After your last line:

1.   Hold the moment for a couple of beats (Cutting Point 1)
2.   Hold the moment for a couple of beats, then shift your focus (Cutting Point 2)

3. Hold the moment for a couple of beats, shift your focus, and then look back to the other character (Cutting Point 3).

Scene 17.1

A Student and Professor are seated in the professor's office.

PROFESSOR

Three students came to me and reported that you cheated on the final exam.

STUDENT

(beat)
What? Are you serious?

PROFESSOR

Yes.

STUDENT

Well, I didn't cheat.

PROFESSOR

Then why did they come to me and say that you did?

STUDENT

I don't know.

PROFESSOR

Did you cheat on the final exam?

STUDENT

I can't believe you are asking me this.

PROFESSOR

It is my job to –

STUDENT

Who were they? They accuse me and you just believe them?

PROFESSOR

I didn't say that I –

> STUDENT
>
> Then why are you looking at me like that?
>
> PROFESSOR
>
> Because it is my job to investigate when something has been reported.
>
> STUDENT
>
> Well, I didn't. And I don't appreciate your accusations.
>
> There is an uncomfortable silence between the two of them.
>
> *End of scene.*

Analysis

The circumstances and conflict of the scene are clear. The professor is confronting the student about cheating on the final exam, and they're denying it. The scene escalates as the professor applies pressure, and the student pushes back, defending their innocence. If you are playing the student, what could you do in the final beat to give the editor multiple cutting options? After the last line, "I don't appreciate your accusations," hold the moment for a beat. This way you give the editor a nice picture of tension between the two characters. After you hold the moment, shift your focus. Stay in the moment and connect the movement to what your character is feeling. On your focal shift, the editor can cut to the professor or stay on you. If the editor cuts to the professor, they have another option to cut back to you when your focus shifts back to the professor. If you freeze, you have given the editor only one option. Why not give them two or three more? The editor can still use the first moment for the end of the scene if they choose, but now they have multiple options to make the scene more dynamic. If the director hasn't called cut, keep acting. Hold the final beat, shift your focus, and give them more cutting points.

Exercise 17.1

- Prepare the role of the student and have a partner play the role of the professor.
- Practice holding the last moment for a beat or two.

- Give a focal shift away from the professor and then back to them.
- Combine these techniques with the emotional life of the character.
- Shoot the scene in a medium close-up and play the footage back to see the cutting points.

Use the Prop

One way to create an exciting acting moment at the end of the scene is by using a prop. As discussed in Chapter 14, Physical Continuity, ask yourself, "How can I use my prop to express what my character is feeling?" When you use a prop to put the finishing touch to the end of a scene, it creates believable behavior that provides the editor more cutting options. The action should be specific, and it must always be connected to what the character is feeling.

Analysis

Now imagine that you are playing the role of the professor. There are a stack of papers and a pen on your desk. How could you use the props to create a dynamic ending? After the student says, "And I don't appreciate your accusations":

1. Hold the moment of tension between the two of you for a couple of beats.
2. Then, look down as you grab the pen.
3. Then, give a stare back to the student as you begin to work on the papers.
4. Then, slowly set the pen down and look back to the student, expressing how you feel in the moment.

This way, the editor could cut the scene during the intense stare or multiple other ways after that. You created a physical action that strengthens the story and makes your performance more interesting.

Exercise 17.2

- Learn the role of the professor and get a partner to play the role of the student.
- Practice holding the last moment for a beat or two.

- Use the pen and papers to create a strong ending with multiple cutting points.
- Shoot the scene in a medium close-up and play the footage back to see the cutting points.

Beats Again?

As we discussed in Chapter 12, The Art of the Reaction, a *beat* marked by the screenwriter indicates a brief pause and shift in emotion between the characters. It usually comes after a tense moment or when a character pauses in thought. An editor will often cut for a reaction here because something is happening between the two characters in the silence.

Analysis

Notice the marked beat at the beginning of the scene, after the professor says, "Three students came to me and reported that you cheated on the final exam." If you are playing the role of the student, how could you play the beat? Would you look at the professor when they say their first line, "Three students came to me and reported that you cheated on the final exam," and then react by looking away? Would you start by looking away and then react by shifting your focus back to the professor after their line? Could you incorporate using a prop? Here are some options:

1. Start the scene by looking down at a prop (smartphone) and then shift your focus to the professor after their line.
2. Start the scene by looking at the professor, hold the beat after their line, then look down at your smartphone.

Depending on your choices, both of these would be strong options. Use these techniques to inspire your choices and combine them with the *character's world*.

Chapter Notes

- Hold the last moment for a couple of beats.
- If the director hasn't called "Cut," keep acting.
- Focal shifts at the end of the scene will provide cutting points and add dimension to the scene.
- Focal shifts should be spontaneous and connected to what your character is feeling.
- When you shift your focus away from the other character, shift back to your original focal point.
- Use a prop to provide options to cut on physical action and strengthen the moment.

PART THREE
THE PROFESSIONAL WORLD

18

AUDITIONING

Mindset

What do you value when you audition? Once you are clear on this, you will reduce any unnecessary pressure that you have put on yourself. You will begin to enjoy the audition experience. Are you concerned with being liked? Thought of as the most brilliant actor in the history of the world? Hoping that the casting director will love you? If these thoughts run through your mind from time to time, you are not alone. However, they aren't going to help you in your audition. Focus on what you can control and not what is out of your hands. You may or may not get the job, and that's fine, because actually you are not there to get the job. Of course, you want the job; we all want the job. You may get it, but you will never be able to control that outcome. If you put pressure and expectations on yourself to book the job, the only thing you will gain is unnecessary stress and anxiety. What if you decide to seek your own applause instead of the acceptance of the casting director? What if you shift your mindset to valuing your preparation? What if you focus on learning your lines, committing to the character, and playing a strong objective? Those are things that you can control. If you put your attention on those areas, the rest will fall into place. You are there to show your skill and what makes you unique. Focus on the joy of being the best actor you can be and you will relieve any pressure that you've created in your mind. You will find freedom in front of the camera. Define your success by the things that are in your control. Write down specific goals for each audition and you will be amazed at how quickly you improve. Remember, the part is yours for the next 5 minutes, so enjoy it!

Practice Improves Everything

When I first moved to New York City, I decided that I wanted to improve at auditioning. I challenged myself to go on every open call for theatre, film, or television that I could attend, with no desire to get the job. I had convinced myself that I wasn't going in to book a job. I had different goals. I was there to get comfortable in the room, build relationships, and find the joy in auditioning. I set up a system where I would give myself measurable goals. Some of them were committing to the objective of the character, remembering to breathe on camera, delivering a confident slate, or focusing on a specific moment. After every audition, I would write down in my journal the date, name of the project, casting director, and a brief assessment of my work in the room. This method led to paid jobs down the road. The most enlightening discovery I made during this experiment, was that I felt free in the room and actually had fun auditioning! I felt good about my work, received many callbacks, booked some jobs, and developed relationships with wonderful people. I attribute this to the fact that I wasn't going into the audition to "get" the job. I had other goals in mind, which freed me from the pressure or expectation of landing the role. The moment you get ahead of yourself and think, "If I get this job then I will …" or "I have to do great because …" you stop living in the moment.

Professionalism

It is important to always be on time for your auditions. Casting directors operate on a tight schedule, and their time should be respected. However, emergencies happen. If you are late, briefly explain your situation and thank them for their patience. Stay positive and don't ever blame anyone or argue.

No matter how you feel about your audition, always thank the casting director for seeing you. Take a moment and make eye contact with them.

This small gesture will go a long way in your career. You will have good and bad auditions. That is just part of being an actor. Stay positive and continue to focus on your specific goals. Casting directors are well aware that you won't have the perfect audition each time. However, they will take note of your preparation and attitude.

Nerves

The best way to reduce performance anxiety is preparation. However, even when we do prepare, we may find that we are still nervous. This happens to just about everyone, and to be a little nervous is good. Nerves can keep your energy in sharp focus and can help your audition. Shift your focus off yourself and channel your nerves into what you want in the scene. Often, we get nervous when we are about to reveal ourselves, and that is what makes a great actor. This feeling is your talent coming through. So, shift your mindset and consider the nerves a gift. It is helpful to accept your nerves and not try to fight them. You may even have a fun mantra for when you feel your nerves kick in, such as, "Oh, I'm nervous. Awesome!" It may sound silly, but it works. Another technique is to take a few deep breaths and put your attention on something outside of yourself. It can help to take your attention off yourself and focus on a physical object in the room. Also, something that I have found to be enormously freeing when dealing with nerves is to say to myself in my mind, "I am going to have fun doing this right now." This is something that you can tell yourself right before you audition.

Dress Like the Character

"What should you wear for your audition?" It depends on the role, but there some general guidelines that you should consider for any on-camera audition. You want to look appropriate for the character and never wear a costume. Wear clothes that you look great in that hint at the character. If you are wearing something that appears to be a costume, it will be a challenge for them to focus on your audition. This tends to make you look more like an amateur than an actor. There are always exceptions, but, as a general rule, dress like the character on a good day and avoid the costume look. Casting directors are creative and they have an imagination, if you allow them to use it.

Make it as easy as possible for the casting director to immediately see you as the character. The last thing I want to do is stifle anyone's creativity, but it's important to pay close attention to how film and television dress characters. How does the current media industry define these looks? You want the casting director to quickly believe that you are the character. Let's look at a couple of examples for specific character types. These are only ideas and not a list of prescriptive rules of how to dress for your audition. They are meant to inspire you. Hopefully, they will get your imagination moving in a positive direction.

If you are auditioning for a doctor, how can you dress without wearing a lab coat and stethoscope around your neck? Think about doctors' profession and social status. They work in a knowledge-intensive field. We tend to view them as professional, caring, and often wealthy. So, how could you give that impression in an audition? You could wear nice slacks, a button-down shirt or blouse with the sleeves rolled up. Why roll up the sleeves? Well, doctors are dealing with sick patients all day and they are often washing their hands. Maybe you wear a nice watch or bracelet. If you were walking down the street dressed in that wardrobe, I doubt anyone would say, "Hey, what's with the doctor's costume?"

A current character type is the *millennial hipster*. Hipsters are part of a subculture that represents authenticity and style. The next time you are in a cool coffee shop, notice the fashion style of the baristas and many of the customers. Hipsters often wear layered clothing, dark skinny jeans, oversized sweaters or flannels, rimmed glasses, cool fedora-style hats, or knit beanies, and some have beards or unique facial hair. Observe other people and have fun creating your version of the character.

What Works

Solid colors that bring out your best features are always a good approach. Do some research and find out what colors look best on you. Run a test and try those clothes out on camera and see what you prefer. Talk to your friends and family, because they will have a helpful opinion on which colors make you "pop." You want your on-camera audition to look dynamic. So, find the colors that complement your skin tone and bring out your best qualities. A helpful tip is to google images of models from your favorite clothing stores that have a similar look or skin tone as you. How are they dressed? What color combinations are they wearing? Professional designers get paid a lot of money to dress models. Use their work as a resource.

What to Avoid

Busy patterns, stripes, and logos may be distracting for the casting director. Instead of watching your performance, they will be focused on the brand on your shirt. You are the brand that is being advertised, and everything should support you. Busy patterns or fine stripes can cause a strange optical phenomenon called the moiré effect. It will create a separate animated pattern on your clothing that can be very distracting. Also, bright neon colors and solid white often bounce too much light on camera and should be avoided.

Have It on "Standby"

Have a couple of audition outfits ready and waiting in the wings. I find it helpful to have these outfits hanging in the closet, set aside for auditions. In a sense, they are your "audition uniform." When you have an audition pop up (and they will), your clothes are waiting for you on "standby." You already know that they look good on you. This will alleviate any stress as you quickly prepare for your audition. Psychologically, it will help you get into "game mode." It will put you in a good headspace in the way that works for an athlete when they put on their uniform before the match. It gives your mind a simple reminder that you are letting go of what has happened and focusing on the task at hand. It will send a signal to your body and prepare it for the job that you are about to do. So, try having a few "go-to" audition outfits and, of course, try new looks to find what works best for you.

The Slate

An audition slate is when you introduce yourself directly into the camera lens before you play the scene. Many casting directors will have you slate your name, height, and the name of the character directly into the camera. You don't need to slate "in character" either. For example, if you are auditioning for a dangerous character, you don't need to prove that you are the character in your slate by being threatening. Remember that you are an actor and you're there for a job interview. However, you can slate by giving the feeling and energy of the character. In general, be pleasant and friendly. After your slate, shift into the world of the character before you begin the scene. The ability to transform, in a moment, from actor to character is how you want to be remembered. For commercials, the slate is usually your name, height, and anything specific to the spot that may be needed. For example, you may need to answer if you can drive a car or if you are allergic to dogs. If they don't give you specific directions, stick with your name and height.

Questions?

Casting directors will often ask you if you have any questions about the scene. I recommend politely answering no to this question, unless you are confused about a major circumstance of the storyline. For example, you may ask, "Am I talking to my mother in this scene?" or "Did my character lose their child?" These are legitimate questions, but I wouldn't get into your specific choices for the character because nobody knows how the scene will eventually be played. At this point, it's best to stick with your choices. The casting director wants to see your interpretation of the character. If you get into a discussion about the specifics of how to play the scene before you've tried one take, you will be throwing out all of the work that you prepared by quickly trying to adjust. I have found it useful to ask the casting director if you are on the right track after you have read the scene. They may say, "Yes, that's the right idea." Or they may give you specific direction: "Try it again, and fight more for the custody of your child this time." Great! You've done the scene once the way you prepared and now you get an opportunity to do it again with their direction. If they give you direction, that means that they like what you are doing. So, listen carefully and go for it.

Chapter Notes

- Create a rubric of the things you can control in your audition.
- Write down specific goals for each audition.
- Focus on the joy of auditioning, and not on getting the job.
- Practice auditioning to improve.
- Dress like the character, but don't wear a costume.
- Channel your nerves into the scene, because they are a gift.
- The slate is delivered directly into the camera.
- Stick with the choices that you have prepared first.

19

LEARN FROM THE PROS

The Audition Reader

Sometimes, the reader is the casting director or the assistant, but often it's an actor who is building a relationship with that casting director. It's a good idea to introduce yourself to the reader and quickly check in with them. It only takes a moment and it can really help your audition. If you connect with them, they will be present with you when you play the scene. A simple gesture to connect with them and make them feel valued can make a huge difference. You may even ask them a small favor. For example, if the reader has the first line of the scene, you could ask them to give you a few moments before they say their first line. This allows you to play the scene the way that you have prepared, and it will help you form a bond with the reader before you play the scene.

Pro Tip 1

I was fortunate to be the audition reader for a few Hollywood films. I had the opportunity to observe many well-known actors in the audition room. On one particular film, I remember the final callback audition with a recognizable actor. It was toward the end of a long day when he came in. The casting director introduced him to the director, producers, and the reader (me). This actor had charisma and, in about 60 seconds, he quickly won over the room. The director was ready to film the scene with both of us performing off-book and on-camera. Before we started, this actor asked if he could have a quick private moment with me. Me? Who am I? I am just the reader. What could he possibly want from me? I will never forget what he did. He took me aside, lowered his voice, and gave me a quick pep talk. He asked me to not hold back in the scene and really go for it. Then he looked me in the eye and said, "I need you, man." This all took less than a minute, and it's a moment that I will never forget. I had never met him before and haven't spoken with him since. However, on that day, I felt so connected to him and excited to be his scene partner. He made me, the reader, feel important, and he booked the job.

Breathe

Breath is one of your most powerful assets. When you are connected to your own breath, you can be present with the reader, the character you are playing, and the camera. Before you start your audition, take a couple of deep breaths in through the nose and out through the mouth. This little habit will do wonders for your work in auditions. Don't ever be embarrassed about taking a breath or feeling that it is somehow a sign of weakness. It's not at all. I have seen many actors whom I have admired on film and television for years take a deep breath before they begin the scene in their audition. If they do it, it may be a good idea. I appreciate these little subtle reminders that we are all human. Take a moment and actually feel your waistline be moved by your breath. When your breath is centered, you will be able to look not *at,* but *into* your scene partner.

Pro Tip 2

I was an audition reader for a feature film with an accomplished and well-trained actor. I have admired her since I first saw her perform on Broadway many years ago. She has an extensive résumé including a Tony Award, a Golden Globe Award, and an Academy Award nomination. The day I read with her, I learned a lot in a brief amount of time. For her audition, she was in a medium close-up shot seated across from me. I noticed that she took a slow, conscious, deep breath before she began the scene. What I experienced over the next 60 seconds was a master class, and it has left a great impression on me to this day. Many actors look *at* you when they play a scene, and there is a self-consciousness as they rate their own performance. She was the opposite. She was connected to her breath. She looked *into* me as she read the scene. When someone is that present, it can be a bit startling. It feels like they are speaking to your soul. She had her attention focused completely on me and silently demanded that I be present with her. I learned a valuable lesson that day. Take a breath before you begin, feel your breath move your waist, and look *into* the reader.

Prepare

Pro Tip 3

The one common theme that I have noticed from all of the working actors that I have seen audition is their thorough preparation. I will never forget the day that I was a reader for a big-budget feature film and a recognizable actor came in to audition. This is an actor who has been successful in the business for over 30 years, with more than 50 feature film credits. In fact, I was surprised that an actor of his caliber even had to audition. At the time, he was performing eight shows a week in a popular off-Broadway play. He came in on a Monday, the normal day off for actors working in the theatre, and he auditioned with two scenes, each three pages long. He was completely off-book. If the director had suddenly told him that they were going to shoot the film that day, he could have. He was that prepared. As I sat there behind the camera filming his audition, I thought to myself, "If he prepares like this for an audition, how dare I not?" As the months rolled on, I noticed that he wasn't the only one out there like that. There were many actors as prepared, but not as famous … yet. It's impossible to give a great audition when you don't know the lines. Prepare and give yourself the best opportunity to succeed. As soon as you get the audition sides, study them and find strong choices that excite you to play the character. I can guarantee you that there are plenty of actors out there doing just that.

The Director's Adjustments

Professional actors have the ability to play the scene multiple ways. I have seen many pros take a note and instantly incorporate it. It takes time to develop this skill, but work toward it. If a director gives you an adjustment in an audition, they are interested in your work. It doesn't mean that they don't like your choices. It usually means the opposite. It's a compliment. Often, they want to see what kind of actor that they will be working with on set – an actor who has many choices and is flexible, or an actor who can only play the scene one way. I have seen many auditions where the actor struggles with making the adjustment. "Try it again but be more subtle." "Try charming her." "Play it like you are in a crowded restaurant." And the actor crumbles. It's concerning to a director if you have only one way of playing the scene and are inflexible. Prepare multiple choices so that you have options in your audition. Listen carefully to the director when they give you an adjustment. If you aren't clear with what they are asking you to do, politely let them know before you start. There can be a lot of emotion and excitement when you are in an audition with the director. It's important to listen with intention and make the adjustment. Film director Lanre Olabisi (*August the First* – Showtime/Netflix, *Somewhere in the Middle* – Netflix, *A Storybook Ending* – HBO) said this:

Whenever you are in an audition, if the director gives you a note, make sure that whatever you do – you give them something different. If you don't understand the note, feel free to ask them to clarify. If it's still not clear, do something – do anything that is different than what you did the first time. Take a risk. Make a choice that is different … one that makes you stand apart from everyone else.

Chapter Notes
- Take a moment to connect with the reader before you start the scene.
- Take a couple breaths to center yourself and focus.
- Look into the reader and not at them.
- Prepare the scene with multiple choices so that you can adjust.
- Listen closely to feedback and make the adjustment.

20

TEN AUDITION TIPS TO HELP YOU WIN

Ten Audition Tips to Help You Win

1. Learn your lines.
   - It's impossible to act when you don't know your lines. The casting director wants to watch you and not the top of your head while you look down for your next line in the script.
   - *Winning Tip*: If you don't have to think about your lines, you will be confident and find freedom playing the scene.
2. Take a moment to live as the character before the first line of dialogue.
   - Your initial thoughts give immediate insight into the character's inner world and excite the viewer about what is to follow.
   - *Winning Tip*: If you crystalize in your mind the events that happened just before your first line, it will inform your performance and fuel the scene.
3. Play a strong objective.
   - Pursue what your character wants from the other character in the scene.

- *Winning Tip*: An audience leans forward to watch when your character is trying to get something from the other character.

4. Embrace the conflict between the characters in the scene.
   - It's exciting to see the character struggle to overcome their problem. If their goal is easy to achieve, it will be boring to watch.
   - *Winning Tip*: If you bring the conflict into the scene, it will strengthen your character's objective.

5. Create an arc for your character.
   - Identify what your character's emotional state is at the end of the scene. Begin the scene in the opposite, or a different, emotional place.
   - *Winning Tip*: If you begin the scene in a different emotional state than the ending, your character will have an arc. They will be more compelling to watch because they will evolve.

6. Listen and react to important information that advances the story.
   Actively listen to the other character and react to key information.
   - *Winning Tip*: The camera never blinks. How you react to key information is as important as when you are speaking.

7. Play the transition in the scene.
   - Play the major transition when your character has an epiphany and their perspective shifts. Look for it toward the end in the last beat of the scene.
   - *Winning Tip*: Playing the transition will allow the audience to see your character change, and they will be interested to see what is going to happen next.

8. Hold the final beat at the end of the scene.
   - Hold the final beat of the scene and then break the tension with a focal shift. Shift your focus back to the

reader to end on a strong moment. Connect the focal shift to the spontaneous emotional state of the character.

- *Winning Tip*: Having a strong final moment will leave a lasting impression.

9. Play an opposite.
   - If the scene is dramatic, find a moment of humor. If it's a comedy, find a serious moment.
   - *Winning Tip*: Playing an opposite will add a surprise to your performance. It will make your character more human, and you will distinguish your audition by not playing the obvious choice.

10. Have empathy for your character and their circumstances.
    - See the world through your character's eyes. Never judge your character. Be sensitivity to their situation and offer a piece of yourself to the character.
    - *Winning Tip*: Every time you play a character you are giving a voice to the people in the world who are experiencing that situation right now. You are speaking for those who would otherwise be silenced. Having empathy for your character's situation is one of the strongest assets you have.

21
INDUSTRY INTERVIEWS

Nidra Sous la Terre (fka Nedra McClyde)

Nidra holds an MFA from the Actors Studio Drama School. She has appeared on Broadway in *The Book of Mormon* and *Marvin's Room* and on television in two seasons of *Orange Is the New Black*, *Instinct*, *Random Acts of Flyness*, *Elementary*, *Bull*, *Jessica Jones*, *30 Rock*, *NCIS: New Orleans*, *Evil*, and *Law and Order: Criminal Intent* (www.nidrasouslaterre.com).

Where did you receive your actor training?

I went to the University of Richmond for my undergraduate degree. I was pre-med because I wanted to be a doctor, and I had received a science scholarship. As they were interviewing me, they saw on my application that I had done a lot of theatre, and I told them, "I'm going to minor in theatre and maybe be a singing doctor." They all laughed, and I got the scholarship. I eventually switched my major from pre-med to theatre and was cast in a play at the Barksdale Theatre in Richmond. There was a moment where I had to cry … and I couldn't. My director tried to teach me little tricks, and something in me said, "I don't want to fake this moment." And it hit me, I didn't know how to act. So, I went back to one of my professors and I said, "I want to go to graduate school to learn how to act." I decided

Figure 21.1 Nidra Sous la Terre (fka Nedra McClyde). (Photo by David Noles Photography.)

on the Actors Studio Drama School, and that is where I learned how to be truthful. It opened me up, and The Method was exactly what I needed. I started doing graduate student films at Columbia and NYU to learn how to put my training to use. I would watch my footage, which everyone hates to do, but I knew this was how I was going to learn.

What are the differences between acting on stage versus camera?
One: rehearsal. Two: timing. And three: you can't edit in theatre. The quality of the prep time before you actually act is so much better in the theatre, and there are fewer unknown factors, but in film and television, it's up to the actor to do a whole lot of the work at home. Once you arrive on set, you have to sneak in moments of rehearsal for yourself. There's rehearsal for camera and lighting … and you have to use that time for yourself. Sometimes on set I will just ask, "Can I have 30 seconds to practice with this prop before we go for a take?"

In the theatre you have this flow of action where you can live for two hours as a character. But you don't have that time on camera, so you often have to plot out what that timing is, so by the time everyone on set is ready to go, you're ready to act. I like to start my moment before prior to "Action" so that by the time the camera is rolling, I'm ready.

When I did *The Book of Mormon* last year, I messed up at least six times before I was flowing. I was dancing a lot and dealing with a lot of props like pitchforks and all sorts of stuff. One night my pitchfork went flying off stage and an audience member in the front row picked it up and handed it to me. I gave him a nod and a wink at curtain call, because he had looked out for me. In film and television, if you mess up, you cut and start over, but you still don't get to live the whole thing. In theatre, you get to mess up, live your life, and try it again eight times a week. After a few weeks, you're like, I got this, and I know how to be a great actor within these circumstances. In film and television, after you get five takes, you're moving on. You're like, "Oh crap, I was not present at all." You lose rhythm in film and television. You have to be ready and not ready all the time which can be nerve-racking. (laughs) Especially if you are working on a scene where the stakes are emotionally high. You have to know how to get yourself there ... maybe in a matter of seconds. You may have to let that emotion sit under the surface for two hours. It's tricky, but that's the craft.

So, you will sneak in extra rehearsal time?

I try to find my little moments of rehearsal. I quickly introduce myself, and I figure out my blocking. I look around the set to see what I might trip on and what might be familiar to my character. Is there some action I do in the scene that is an action that my character might do several times a week? If it's opening this door, let me open this door twelve times, because it's supposed to be familiar to me. I want to know where the camera is going to be, so that I can figure out how to best use my eyeline during this scene. Where's the table? The chair? Let me pull out the chair. It's tricky to get that all in, because there are so many people trying to do their job at the same time. Everyone's job is so important, but I'm like running around, "Sorry, I'm in your way!" There is so much to take in and your brain can be overloaded when it should actually be making space for the craft. So, yes: I sneak in as much time as I can to prevent any uncertainty getting in the way when I need to focus.

Do you have a tip about being on set?

As an African American woman, I have learned to take more control of my own makeup and hair. In the beginning of my career, I didn't know that I could do that. I would see myself on camera and think, "Why do I look ashen? Why is my hair jacked up?" That happened several times, and when I started doing student films, I began asking the directors, "Do you mind if I do my own makeup?" They would say, "We've hired someone already who is good. You'll be fine." But it wasn't. Then I got to a point on professional sets where I would come with my foundation already on, and my hair done.

Any other dos or don'ts?

Be early, but not too early. The set is a well-oiled machine and you don't want to arrive too early and throw things off. I like to go to set about 5–10 minutes before call time.

Always bring a phone charger. Bring a book. And, one of your favorite drinks and snacks.

Get to know the PAs, Assistant Director, and always introduce yourself to the DP. The AD is one of the first people that you will meet on set, and they will give you a lot of direction. You want to be able to call them by name if you need something. Sometimes I'll ask the DP, "What shot is this?" Or, "Would it be better if I turn this way?" You are collaborating and working together. It's important to connect with the person who is actually recording you. Or, I may ask the AD between takes if they are watching the monitor. I try to gauge who is least busy.

Do you have a technical tip when acting for the camera?

Knowing how to choreograph your eyes. It's like the frame is the proscenium, and you have to think about the audience being behind the camera lens. Everything that you think and feel is behind your eyes. The more access you give to them the better, which means less blinking and eye shifting. If you want a powerful moment, when you hear an important line, have your gaze slightly down and then look up to the character and camera. It's a powerful move. I want fluidity and ease, but I practice, especially with self-tapes at home, how powerful I can be with my eyes. They are the most valuable tool for the camera. The more purposeful and still we can be with them, the more we allow the audience to see us.

What is a big challenge for you on camera?
Blocking out all of the distractions that keep me from being focused and present. Acting asks us to put our imagination in overdrive. You have to pretend that there isn't a giant pole with a fluffy microphone above your head, a mic pack jabbing your back, and twelve people standing around staring at you. You have to pretend that you are in a real building and not a set that someone built. I find that using that part of my imagination can take away from using my imagination for my character. To combat that, I do a lot of breathing. I will come back to my breath to be present with myself. Also, I try to have some dialogue with my scene partner. I want to establish that it's us in this world and not everything else. "Last looks" is when hair, makeup, and wardrobe come rushing to set to see if you look good right before "Action" is called, and I may need to think about the car accident that just happened. It's good to be thinking the character's thoughts during "last looks" instead of my own thoughts.

Any tips about auditioning?
It's empowering to have your own plan, and the outcome of that plan is in your hands. If you think in terms of wanting to get the job, you're giving someone else the power to make a decision about you. But, if you go into the room and focus on being a really good actor, it's in your control, and it's easier to let go of what is not in your control.

That's so true. It's best to focus on offering your best work and not just wanting the job.
I know! Why doesn't anyone teach this? I'm doing my best to teach it to my students, but why didn't anyone say this to us when we were students? "Don't worry about the job, worry about being a really good

actor"? That's what they want! You've got to keep doing great work and eventually the universe will align for you. It always does.

What advice do you have for a young actor?

Every young actor wants to work and be famous, but what I think is more important is legacy. When you're on your deathbed, what is the work that you did that you are proud of? Did I do the work that I wanted to do with my life? It would have been great as a young actor if I thought more about the type of work that I wanted to do. Being super clear with *why* I want to be an actor. What do I want to leave for other people, when I leave this Earth? As a young actor, you could be saying five lines, handing another actor a glass of water and feel, "This is not fulfilling at all." But if you know in your heart that it is leading to the work that you want to do someday, it will make the journey worthwhile. You will be less frustrated and dissatisfied, because you know your trajectory. I'm not saying that, at 19 or 21, you should be saying no to a role just because it won't get you an Oscar. But, it's important to know what kind of work excites you and where your spirit is leading you. It's empowering to have your plan, and the outcome of your plan is in your hands.

Jason Liles

Jason is an actor who is most known for his performance capture roles. He played George opposite Dwayne Johnson in the movie *Rampage*, Ryuk in *Death Note*, and King Ghidorah in *Godzilla: King of the Monsters*.

What is motion capture acting?

It's just acting, like you would do for any role, but with many cameras recording your performance and transferring it into a character model on a computer. Motion capture is capturing the movement of your head and body, and performance capture records the movement of your face, hands, and fingers. People use the terms interchangeably, but my performances in movies like *Rampage* are actually performance capture.

Figure 21.2 Jason Liles. (Photo by David Muller Photography.)

How does it work?

It's kind of like digital makeup. You wear a suit with wires and these little dots all over it, and there is a grid with 20–30 cameras throwing out infrared light on you. It bounces off of the reflective metallic dots on your suit and is captured in real time into the computer. So, for *Rampage*, they took my performance and put it into the model of George. That's why you can look at a shot of me next to George and go, "Oh my god, that's Jason!"

How do you approach a role like George?

Like any other role on camera. I focus physically, vocally, and psychologically on the character. I am thinking about being George, being a gorilla. I approach the character and the beats in the script like any other character.

How did you get into performance capture?

I didn't try to. I was just an actor who got an opportunity. I trained in college, at the New York Film Academy, and all over New York City for six years. I moved to LA and never thought I would do performance capture because I am 6' 9". Then, I suddenly got an opportunity to play Ryuk in *Death Note*. Then, Colin Strauss, the visual effects supervisor on *Death Note*, asked me at a barbecue, "Hey, Jason, what do you know about gorillas?" I'm like, "Uhhh, I don't know." He told me that he was doing *Rampage* with The Rock, and they were looking for someone taller than Dwayne Johnson to play George, so that he would have to look up in some of the scenes. Because we worked well together on *Death Note*, Colin recommended me as his top guy. I went in for a meeting with Terry Notary, who trained Josh Brolin and Mark Ruffalo in *Avengers* and all the actors who played apes in the *Planet of the Apes*. Terry's the greatest. He wanted to work with me, and we started training.

How did you train?

We worked every day for weeks in the Santa Monica Mountains to get into the mind of a gorilla. He helped me strip away Jason and become George. He guided me through meditations and told me, "Let your mind sit in a hammock." I watched a lot of documentaries, and I drew a lot from Koko, the gorilla who had learned sign language from Dr. Francine Patterson. The given circumstances are that George has been saved from poachers and raised by Davis, Dwayne Johnson's character, for seventeen years. He's taught him sign language and they're like brothers. It's a similar relationship to Dr. Patterson and Koko. Also, I would study gorillas at the zoo for months. They are so present, alive, and they own their space. In the end, we discovered that George is just a big kid. He loves to play, and his objective is to make people laugh. He loves that!

Any other inspirations?

I watched a lot of interviews with Andy Serkis, who did performance capture for Gollum in *Lord of the Rings* and *The Hobbit* and [for

Caesar in] *Planet of the Apes*. What I kept hearing from him was that there is no difference when acting in performance capture. You're still in front of the camera playing a character.

How was working on the set?
Terry taught me how to get into character on set. He told me that when someone says, "Hey Jason," and you don't want to respond because you are in the mind of George, you know you're ready. I wouldn't look at my phone and when I heard cut, I would go back to my first position, ready for the next take. The first day I worked with Naomi Harris. We didn't meet until after we had worked together for twelve hours. I went up to her afterwards, like a little kid, and said, "Hi Naomi, I'm Jason! It's so nice to work with you!"

What is challenging about working in performance capture?
Technically, you have a camera attached to your face hanging off the end of your nose, and it's easy to forget it's there. You start bumping into things, but the biggest challenge is always finding the truth of the character. You have to stay present for every take, because the editors can use all of the material that you give them. There was a moment at the end of the film in *Rampage* of George smiling, but that was from a take I did in the beginning of the film. I was on set every day in a real environment which helped, but, for *Godzilla*, we were in a big warehouse studio like a soundstage called a performance capture volume. We had to imagine everything. In a way it's difficult, but in another way, it's easier because it's pure imagination.

What's most exciting about performance capture?
It's the coolest tool in the world, because you can be any character. It doesn't matter your age, gender, or ethnicity. I can be baby George one moment and then thirty-foot tall George the next. The technology doesn't discriminate. There's no limit. You can be Gollum, King Kong, or anything!

How does a young actor get into performance capture?

Focus on being a great actor, and maybe a role will require performance capture technology. People go to Andy Serkis all the time, but it's not because he's good at performance capture, it's because he's a great actor. So, train and focus on that.

What other opportunities are there?

Many performers who do motion capture for video games come from a stunt, combat, or martial arts background. For those mediums, they need actors who can do all of those kicks, tackles, and handle weapons.

What's your favorite memories of working in performance capture?

Training with Terry and working with Dwayne Johnson. He showed instant respect to me and everyone. On the first day, he said, "We're going to be best buds!" He's so humble, and he always made me feel that my work was important. After we wrapped, Dwayne passed a microphone around to everyone so we could say a few words. I got emotional thanking the team, and he came over and hugged me. He's incredible.

What's your advice to young actors?

Always give back. It never gets old and it's fulfilling. When you're depressed, you tend to focus on yourself, and this business can do that, but the most happy and joyful people help others. If you focus on adding value to people's lives, you'll get a lot in return. Getting to the top of the mountain is a success but getting others to the top is significance.

Jandiz Estrada Cardoso – Casting – Senior Director, Global Talent Development, NBC Universal

Jandiz has worked on pilots and series with networks including AMC, ABC, CBS, Starz, Spike TV, and MTV, and films with feature studios including Disney, WB, Paramount, Universal, New Line, and Screen

Figure 21.3 Jandiz Estrada Cardoso. (Photo by Oscar Moreno.)

Gems. In 2010, she joined NBC Universal's New York casting office, which auditions for all pilots and served as associate on the last season of the Emmy Award-winning series, *30 Rock*. She was voted *Backstage Magazine*'s Reader's Choice Award for Audition Coach of the Year. In 2019, she was the recipient of the Golden Eagle Award for Diversity Impact in Television.

What is the job of the casting director in television?
To find the actor that best tells the story the creators want. On television, that role can be a series regular, guest star, or co-star. Actors coming right out of the gate, their first jobs are usually a co-star. That's the union scale minimum character that comes on for one episode.

That's a role like, "Excuse me, can you please sign this credit card?"
Correct! Sometimes a co-star is a great way for the show to exercise some comedic relief or to reveal a secret. They're fun roles and if you really shine in that moment, you can show that you are ready to step up to recurring co-star or a guest star.

So, a co-star role could lead to more opportunities down the road?
Yes, often the co-stars are written as one-episode characters. But sometimes you impress them, and they write you into more episodes. I've definitely seen some of my actors get written into more episodes because they were so fun in that one moment and then, one episode becomes three or four. Also, it's important to know when you are auditioning for a co-star. Let's say you were auditioning for *30 Rock*, where the leads were Tina Fey and Alec Baldwin. They're allowed to improv, go crazy, and do a lot of zany things, but it's important to know, "Oh, I'm the co-star that's going to set up Alec Baldwin's line." So, I need to give them exactly what they want and nail it. Understanding that really helps you prepare.

How do you find actors?
Well, you know that I am a diehard theatre goer and am devastated by the pandemic [COVID-19]. Right now, I am unable to scout the best actors on stage. Theatre is my favorite way. In Los Angeles and New York, we are lucky because we can go to the theatre every night. I go to comedy clubs a lot, too. Comedy is a big deal where I work, and we like to transition comedians into actors and writers. I go to film festivals like Sundance, but also lesser-known festivals like LA Skins Fest (which is entirely Native Indigenous content creators), American Black Film Festival, LA International Latino Film Festival, and Outfest. I watch a lot of television that may be under the radar, too.

It feels like we're in a time where actors can have more autonomy over their own career by creating their own material.
Absolutely. Contemporary millennial actors are creating a lot of their own shows on YouTube and getting noticed.

Do you have any tips for auditioning in person?
We are not there to look at you for this one role. You are there today to present your choices for this one role, but in actuality, I may be looking at you for other roles. I might be pushing you for a role that you aren't right for because I love how creative you are, and I keep

inviting you back. So, when you come in, I want you to be professional. I want you to be off-book. I don't want to hear any excuses that your train was late or your Uber was this because there are forty other actors outside who are ready to audition. We are your greatest champions. I am bringing you in because I think you could book this role! I just need you to come and seal the deal. I started the conversation, I will continue the conversation, and advocate for you. You need to show up and deliver the goods. Your audition is a gift to the casting director, and if you're good, it's like Christmas morning. And once you give that gift, never question yourself by thinking, "I hope she liked it?" Don't do that to yourself. Once you give that gift, that's it, end of story and move on to the next.

Any tips about the frustration of not booking roles?
When it comes to auditioning, you are going to audition 99% more than when you're going to book a role. It's a numbers game and when you do get a job, you will get paid, but most likely nothing too creative will happen on that day. You'll get two takes and be done. Everything creative happens preparing for the role. The more you love dissecting character and auditioning as opposed to only working, the more you will succeed.

What are some common mistakes that you see actors make?
It all comes down to the preparation. Anything could happen on that day, depending on the reader or other variables, but the only thing that you can control is your preparation. Focus on the choices and, when you think you've found something great, choose something else. Try to come up with five or six great choices and be confident that those are choices that no one else has done. You can pick the obvious choice but go a little deeper and present something unique. When you do that, you will be happy and feel at peace with letting it go. A lot of actors spend three hours committing to one choice, and they get stuck. I give them direction in the room, and they are unbendable. It throws them off. But, if you have prepared six or seven options and I say, "Could you be gentler on that moment with your

father?" You say, "Sure, that was one of my explorations." You'll be able to adjust.

That sounds like a good way to keep it feeling new.
Yeah, and so you have a good time! Actors get into the craft because they want to crawl in and out of different worlds. So, enjoy that process.

Do you have any tips about self-taping?
Tech is very important. Lighting and sound are important. I don't mind if you use your phone, but don't have the camera moving around. Have a simple clean background and don't wear a costume. If you're playing a doctor, you don't need scrubs and a stethoscope. Props are very distracting. It's got to be clean because you don't want anything taking away from your performance. 50% of the self-tapes we see are with the worst readers, and it doesn't help you deliver. So, please develop a community of friends that are accessible, and have them on your speed dial. You have to have an acting buddy that you can trust ... a circle of acting friends.

Any other tips?
Don't put your audition on a site that anyone can view, and have it protected with a password. You should definitely be off-book and send me your best take. I don't want to see four takes. Also, actors need to invest in self-taping equipment. You need a $40 tripod, $40 lights, and you need your friends.

Any advice about websites and social media?
I love a good website that is easy to find. Every actor needs to have their best material searchable online. Otherwise, I am left to see what you have on Twitter and Facebook, and you may not want that. So, direct me to your work that is curated by you. Keep your personal life private. We all know that viewers will use what you put out there as a resource to define you. And, make sure that your name is always the same on the accounts associated with your work. It's a good idea to call SAG-AFTRA to see if your name is already

taken, and then, if needed, you can decide on a different one. Also, make sure that your website is current and working. Many actors have outdated websites that malfunction or are difficult to navigate. It should be crisp, clean, and professional. BIO. GALLERY. VIDEOS. PRESS. CONTACT. Don't put up a reel where the footage is low quality.

It doesn't help you, right?
Correct. Also, if you put up your self-tape audition online, make sure to take it down because it can be copyright infringement.

Any other advice about reels?
Yes, early in your career it's marvelous when people will ask you to work on their projects, even if it's for free. Many college MFA films will go onto festivals and some may even be nominated or win an Academy Award. So, when you go into these submission sites where it says MFA films, a lot of them will be of a very high quality and be a good piece for your reel. That's your goal. Your headshot and résumé are important, but your reel is even more important. You need a few high-quality scenes that speak to your strengths. So, don't shy away from working for free, and always make sure from the beginning that you can get a copy of your work after the project wraps.

What is your overall advice to an actor starting in the business?
If you want to be in this industry, no one else tells you how much you are worth. You have full power over how much you want to give to acting, and it should never be dictated by a paycheck or some timeline. If performing feeds your heart, you will find a way to do it, even with a survival job. If you are lucky enough to realize that you want to be an artist, you won't look at success or failure in that binary way. Acting will give to you what you need from it, and you should enjoy every second of it because it's fun. But, if it stops being fun and becomes a struggle, it's not a sad thing to take a break from it. It's always going to be a hustle, but it should never be a painful grind because you are so much more than that. You are an emotional

vessel that you can tap into, and that will cross over into so many different aspects of your contributions to the world.

That is awesome.
And, be humble. Don't let your ego get in the way by competing with your acting friends or significant other. The best actor doesn't always get the job. So, don't allow not getting a job to define your value.

Kenneth Suarez and Nelson Henderson

Kenneth Suarez and Nelson Henderson are the former owners of Brick Entertainment in Los Angeles, California. They have successfully represented commercial actors for years.

How do you find actors to represent?
Nelson: A variety of ways. We always gave consideration to just about every submission, whether it was electronic, hard copy or a referral.

Figure 21.4 Kenneth Suarez. (Photo by Bettina Niedermann.)

Figure 21.5 Nelson Henderson. (Photo by Bettina Niedermann.)

Our job was to find the best talent to fulfill our needs and meet industry demand. We found the most productive way was through referral.

Would the referrals come from other clients?
Kenneth: Managers that understood our agency and the kind of actor we were looking for, as well as clients, casting directors, directors, writers, and even friends. We believed it paid to at least review every submission due to ever-changing advertising demographics. Some of it depends on the talent agency, too. We represented performers across all demographics, with an emphasis on "aspirational" and "comedic" actors. Other talent agencies may have used different criteria to filter submissions.

Nelson: Since commercials are an entry into the business for many actors, we never discouraged anyone from submitting to us, because we were able to find a lot of diamonds in the rough. However, it's important for actors to present themselves professionally. Some actors submit before they're ready. You can't just have your friend take your picture and say, "I'm ready to be an actor." Do the research. Get informed.

What makes an actor "ready" to submit to you?

Kenneth: Actors with training, headshots that indicate they have an understanding of the medium and are clear about who they are and where they fit. It's helpful if their package (headshots, résumé, and reel) tells a story. Actors who are confident in their abilities seem to have a nose for how the business works and show an interest in building a partnership. We wanted to see the actor's personality come through. The one thing that's inherent in a submission is that the person wants to be an actor. So, take the opportunity to let us know who you are and what you're about. Include a few things that make you unique.

What makes a good client?

Kenneth: A good communicator who's flexible and comes equipped with all, or at least some, of the necessary tools to compete for jobs.

Nelson: The best clients are actors who view the relationship as a collaboration, because they are willing to contribute to the partnership. From headshots to training to experience to networking, they are interested in making themselves a commodity to casting.

What are the necessary tools to compete for a job?

Nelson: Headshots, résumé, training are all important factors. The devil is always in the details. For example, if an actor has great headshots/résumé that specifically represent their type, it empowers us when pitching them to casting directors because they are clearly definable. If "Bob" is a Chris Farley type and has a headshot and improv training to validate that, then we have the ammunition to effectively advocate on "Bob's" behalf.

What about flexibility?

Kenneth: All aspects of the industry move fast and include a level of uncertainty. So, operating in that environment requires flexibility. Commercials reward actors who are "gamers" and are willing to answer the call. The ad agency may have an idea on set, and if the actor can jump in and go for it, it's appealing to the creative team, because it provides them with creative flexibility.

Nelson: Improv actors do great in commercials because the casting director, director, and ad agency often are not sure what they want. They need the actor to help create their vision. Flexibility is also being readily available. You may receive a call in the morning to audition that afternoon. The pros have flexible jobs to subsidize their art. It's a requirement to compete in the business.

How important is the headshot?

Nelson: Probably the most important thing. Casting directors won't click on your shot if it doesn't persuade them. It's your gateway into everything. Your headshots should represent the archetypes that you would play in the commercial world, and it should be very clear to casting directors.

Kenneth: It's the actor's business card. It's a window into your personality and to opportunity. Breakdowns from casting directors describe a specific role, how they dress, and their character in the story. It usually works best when it is a believable representation of that breakdown.

How can you take good headshots for the digital world?

Nelson: Today, submissions are done electronically. Headshots are viewed on a computer in one-by-one-inch squares. Casting directors scroll and click on the ones they want to see. You need a razor sharp, colorful, digital shot. The background should not pull focus from you. It should complement and animate what you are representing.

What about framing in a headshot?

Kenneth: The size of the photo dictates certain parameters, the most important of which is that the decision-makers can actually *see* you on the screen in a thumbnail-sized photo. Facial features, hair, eye color, skin tone … all upon a first, quick glance.

Landscape versus portrait?

Nelson: Specialties like being an athlete may require that they see more of your physicality. In general, the best headshot is head, shoulders, and chest. Don't crop too tight, because your wardrobe can help define your character type.

Kenneth: I could see a landscape photo for your website, a landing page for a casting site, or to complement your IMDB page.

Nelson: For commercial actors, vertical or portrait works best because of the technical format of submissions systems. Landscape or horizontal crops the photo too much.

Are there certain archetypes that you see more frequently today?

Kenneth: If you're watching, advertising and television typically provide us with these answers. A current coveted archetype is the "Hip, Edgy, Stylish Millennial" in their 20s. Next year it might be something different.

Nelson: There are traditional archetypes that are somewhat timeless, but new types are dictated by trends and societal movements.

Kenneth: And, there's always room for comedy no matter your look, age, or ethnicity. If you have the ability to be funny on camera, you're more able to transcend archetypes. Otherwise, "Upscale" is a common archetype and "Working Class" thanks to the success of shows like *The Office*.

What can an actor do to help their career and partnership with their agent?

Kenneth: Remain in touch with who they are as a person and performer while being cognizant of the ebb and flow of the business. Expectations untethered to reality often lead to breakdowns in the agent–client relationship.

Nelson: It's important for actors to continue to live their lives. Experience makes you well-rounded and helps your decision-making. Actors can get caught up in constantly focusing on career and forget to live.

Kenneth: Continuing education is important. A refresher workshop or practicing with your friends on camera might help you discover that you have developed a subtle habit that is preventing you from competing for jobs. It will also provide reps and establish more comfort with the audition process.

Nelson: Stay present. If you are in the business long enough, you will change physically and emotionally. Your type will change. Be aware of that.

Should actors be aware of when to reinvent their brand?

Kenneth: Essentially, yes. An actor doesn't have to do anything if they don't want to, but sometimes when they make an organic change, it helps them come into their own and find themselves again. I think it's important for actors to continually remain as honest with themselves about where they are in their career and what they truly want out of it. This is easier said than done and requires a good deal of self-awareness.

What is your advice to a young actor breaking into the business?

Kenneth: Find the part of the craft that gets you up in the morning and build a community that supports this effort. Let it come to you. Steer clear of living in a world of comparison. Everyone has their own path and timeline. Celebrate others' achievements. They are proof that your aspirations are possible.

Nelson: Upon leaving your institution of training, you quickly realize that it was a small circle, and the professional world is a giant circle. You may think that you can play any kind of role but look at the majority of working actors. They always play the same type of character and that is not a bad thing. So, know exactly who you are, what you represent, and where you fit. The quicker you can define yourself to the decision-makers, the sooner you will start working. Once you are steadily working, then you can afford to expand your range.

Any other advice?

Kenneth: It's important to create a full life. Most of the time an actor spends while pursuing their acting career is not spent acting. The first thing I would suggest when starting out in a new city is to set up your life. Find an apartment, transportation, a community, a job that doesn't drain your soul, and then pursue your passion. With these elements in place, I believe it makes it easier to put your best work forward.

Nelson: Yes, make sure you have an infrastructure in place so you can dedicate the time and energy to your acting career that it deserves. You must be ready when opportunity comes. You never know when it will come again.

Kenneth: And, when you're in touch with what inspires you to perform, people tend to want to work with you, because you are operating from a place of joy. Actors who are in touch with this concept tend to work more and move through the business with a sense of grace.

Nelson: Enjoy the journey! Find the fun in every audition or job and never forget why you want to be an actor.

Stacy Solodkin – Beth Stein Agency (BSA) – Owner

BSA is a boutique talent agency representing actors of all ages for feature film, television, and commercials in Los Angeles, CA. Stacy has owned and operated BSA for over 25 years. Her clients have appeared in many

Figure 21.6 Stacy Solodkin. (Photo by Bettina Niedermann.)

popular films, television series, and commercials. Some of their credits include: *The Mayans, Grey's Anatomy, Brockmire, Helstrom, Dolemite Is My Name, 'black-ish, Home Again, Bad Boys III, NCIS: Los Angeles, Boardwalk Empire, The Conners, Will & Grace, Dear White People, This Is Us, The Glass Castle, Sons of Anarchy,* and *Scandal.*

How does an actor find an agent to represent them?

In my opinion, when you are starting out, the goal should not be about finding an agent. You shouldn't try to find an agent. You should learn how to act. I find that a lot of people just want it "all" to just "happen" right away, and they think, "I got to get an agent!" They end up coming to me too early. I can't do anything with an actor who has no training … unless they are a child. The number one thing that I say to actors who are starting out is to find a good class. Go around to all of your actor friends and ask about classes. Start auditing classes. Find a class that scares you and take that one. It should be a class that is reputable and looks good on your résumé. When I see an actor's résumé with a class that I trust I say, "That's a smart actor." I'm always looking for smart actors who come to town and do their research. Once an actor gets in a class and books some work on their own, I can see that they're viable. That's when you write to someone like me. Today, you can find agents on Instagram and Google. Ask your friends about their agents … ask *how* they got their agent … get a referral. That's how you find an agent.

Anything an actor shouldn't do when looking for an agent?

If I am being honest, I truly hate when actors call me on the phone asking how they can submit to me or whether or not I am taking on new clients. When actors call me on the phone it shows me that they haven't done their research. On my website or Instagram account I have instructions on exactly how to submit. Just Google any agency you are interested in. Everything will come up. Do the research.

How long is your typical contract with an actor at your agency?

Usually, I like actors to give me a year. That said we know pretty quickly if it's not working out. My motto is: I only want happy people around me. I never keep someone if they're unhappy. If a client is unhappy, I want them to fly and soar and find a place to be happy. So, it's pretty simple: my job is to make my clients happy. They're job is to tell me whether they're happy or not. If they're not happy, we try and figure out if we can fix whatever isn't working together. It's truly just like, any other relationship. So, to really answer your question … a contract is as long as we want it to last *together*.

How important is the actor's headshot?

It's the most important thing … besides doing the work and studying your craft. The headshot is your calling card. It is everything. When actors send me bad headshots my heart sinks because I know that they won't get called in from casting. You don't have to spend a boat-load of money to have a good headshot. Some headshots, I take off of my client's Instagram, and they may have paid zero dollars for the photo. The headshots need to look interesting … they need to look different. They need to look grounded like that person has some-thing to say and they need to be real. I can usually tell if someone is a good actor or not from their headshot. I am a big believer in finding a really good photographer and not wasting money shooting with someone just because they are cheap.

Is it helpful for an actor to have a reel?

I will not take on an actor without a reel. Seeing someone's work is the only way to know if they are a good actor or not. The mistake that I see actors make with reels is that they don't lead with their best work, and also, they tend to crowd too many things into a reel. When they do that, any "good" scenes get drowned out by a bunch of filler. I wish actors understood that the résumé shows how much work they have done. The reel is *only* about the work. My answer to almost everything is that it's *always about the work*. It's about the craft. I'd rather see one amazing scene than six one-line roles. Give me a really nice scene. Also, I don't like those places where you go to have scenes made. They often look like you went to a scene place. I think that if actors don't have a reel, they should submit themselves through LA Casting or Backstage or Actors Access to get jobs and to ultimately get a reel. Or do it yourself! I just took on an actor that shot their own project during COVID. It was very well written, shot beautifully, and he's amazing in it! You can do it on your own. Be proactive. You don't need to wait until you've booked work but in the meantime audition as much as you can so you can hopefully create a reel from work you have genuinely booked yourself.

Do you find actor websites useful?
No. I don't really find it useful to get work, but when actors submit to me, I go to them. Usually, actors don't choose the best headshots when they are submitting for representation. If they're interesting enough I will go to their website and start looking through their shots to see if there are better ones. In my opinion I think a website can help you get an agent, but I don't think that it helps you get work.

What makes a good client?
Someone who is self-assured enough to let me do my job. A good client is someone who is constantly working at their craft. Someone who I can tell is energetically engaged in their career. This isn't something that they hope for; this is something that they do. Like every NBA player who is on the court every day, they are … in some way … working on their craft every day. That is my favorite kind of actor. My job is to get them auditions, and their job is to say yes and go on the auditions and then hopefully we make a ton of money together! Sometimes actors sabotage themselves. They get an audition and immediately think up reasons why they aren't right for a role. If I submitted you and casting saw your picture and called you in, go on the audition. The actor's job is not to be the agent or the casting director. My favorite actors are the ones that say yes because we don't say no until we have the power to say no, right? In the beginning, we need to say yes … unless it is nudity or something really bad. I love people who love to go do their art.

Any tips about self-taping?

Self-taping is everything right now because of COVID. You have to actually be good at it. It needs to be bright, and I need to be able to hear you. It's needs to be professional like your headshot. If you have a terrible headshot, it's not going to get you called in. They're going to call in the actor with the headshot that pops, right? Also, with the self-tape, it's best if you present yourself in the most professional way. I have an amazing client that I have had for 15 years. He has a self-tape set-up at his home, but it's not great, even though he's bought all of the equipment. When I send him a really big audition, I ask him to go pay at a studio so that it looks professional because I want us to have the best chance at getting the role. You need to get good at it and there are classes that are offered all over town to help.

What can an actor do to improve their chances of getting acting jobs?

The work. The work. The work. Do the work. I've had some clients that are good … their auditions are good … but they're not *great*. I think one of the pitfalls I see many actors fall into is that they think just because they got their BA or MFA or just finished studying in London that they're done. They think that they know how to do it all. As artists there is always room for growth. Just like in sports you always have to keep training. A story I like to tell is from when I was an actor myself and I was working with Doris Roberts for many months on a movie. At the time, she was in her 70s and she was still putting up scenes in class at night. *That's* an actor. Even though she's working as a series regular on television for years, she's on set reading her scene from a play because she's still putting up work in class. The way you improve your chances is to be a better actor. To be the actor that they can't say no to.

What is your advice to a young actor who is just starting out in the business?

To not allow other people's opinions that don't feel right to you to steer you off your path. To check in with your gut always and to not try to fit yourself into a box. To create your own box! To have enough faith in yourself to know that you bring something unique to the table, and to infuse that uniqueness into your work. To never stop working on your craft. To always be finding material that scares you or take classes that scare you. Find ways to work with other actors who are so good you are afraid to get on stage with them! To have a mindset of *growth* and to constantly be pushing yourself to be better.

PART FOUR
SELF-TAPE LIKE A PRO

22

TODAY'S ACTOR
PRODUCTION SKILLS

You are living in the most exciting time to be an actor working in film and television. There is more opportunity happening all over the world, and you have more access than ever before. You have the ability to be in the driver's seat of your career, if you develop some easily attainable production skills. Every actor today must be able to submit a professional-quality self-tape audition. If technology intimidates you, change your mindset, develop some skills, and learn to love it, or you may be left behind.

The modern actor must be equipped with simple tools to shoot, edit, and submit a professional-quality audition. In today's world, you must go beyond "nailing" the part and have some technical skills with lights, sound, and the camera. Like it or not, you will leave a bad impression if you submit an unprofessional headshot, résumé, or self-tape audition. This is not because the industry is filled with mean people who want to tear you down. In my experience, quite the opposite is true. The industry, specifically casting directors and agents, is filled with wonderful people who love actors. Many of them were successful actors earlier in their careers. They know what you are going through and they are on your side. They want you to succeed. They are dying to find the right actor for the job and they want to discover you. However, it's important to remember that their career and reputation are on the line as much as yours. Follow their directions and show them that you are ready to work with them on a professional level. I have worked with many casting directors and agents in my career, and some of them are my closest friends. In fact, they were helpful in writing this book. Believe me, they love talking about how they discovered an actor and helped build their career. You booking a job is exciting for them too.

Whether you are auditioning live in a casting director's office or submitting a self-tape audition, your first contact with the casting director should leave a positive impression. It's important to be professional in every aspect of your work, and the self-tape submission is at the top of the list. Get creative, develop some production skills, and make self-taping fun. If you approach the self-tape audition with this attitude, you will build more confidence in your abilities and find more success. For a small investment, you can build your own professional self-tape studio at home, and Chapters 23 and 24 show you how.

23

STUDIO SPACE

FIND IT NOW

Find your space to self-tape now. Don't wait to get an audition and then panic to find a location. Wherever you may be living, you need to secure an area where you can self-tape that is easily accessible, quiet, and without visual distractions. Be creative and experiment with different areas to see which space is ideal. In each location, record mock auditions at different times of the day to check the lighting and sound. Your self-tape room doesn't have to be an elaborate set or studio that is solely dedicated to your self-tape auditions. It can be an area that you can quickly assemble and self-tape. This can be in a home office, living room, garage, or even a closet (don't laugh … I've seen it done before!). Consider even a common area in an apartment building or dormitory or a theatre space at your university. Reach out to actors within your community and work together. Form a team and help each other out.

Accessibility

Make sure that you have easy access to your self-tape studio. For example, if you are at a university and you don't have access to the studios in your theatre department at night or on the weekends, then find a Plan B. If you have a roommate who gets up early for work, then maybe auditioning for an intense dramatic scene at night in the living room could present a problem. If you live in an apartment, it will serve you well to let your neighbors know that you are an actor (after you sign the lease ... of course!). Let them know when you are auditioning with a loud or intense scene. Be respectful of others and find a space that you can access at just about any time day or night.

Silence Is Golden

Random background noise is distracting and delivers an amateur self-tape audition. It is not good to submit an audition with the sound of a train running over your most important line of dialogue, the neighbors arguing upstairs when you deliver the punch line, or a dog barking in the background as a tear rolls down your face. These noises will be frustrating for you and the casting director. So, do some research, run some test auditions, and find a space that is quiet. Depending on where you live, this may be challenging. Get creative and don't give in to self-taping in a noisy space by thinking that it's good enough. There are some ways to help improve the sound quality in any space. Rooms with carpets and drapes enormously improve sound quality when filming. Hardwood or tiled floors will create an undesirable echo. If you are experiencing this in your space, try putting some rugs or blankets on the floor to deaden the sound. A quick way to test the sound quality is to clap in the space – if you hear a lengthy echo, it is not ideal. Air conditioners, heaters, fans, clocks, phones, and refrigerators/appliances can also cause unwanted sound in your self-tape audition. So, make sure you turn off anything that is making a sound when you are recording. (And remember to turn it back on afterwards!)

The Backdrop

Like a headshot, you want to be the focus and star of your self-tape audition. This means that you should be in a medium close-up (chest up) frame, well lit, and not upstaged by the background. Avoid submitting a self-tape audition with furniture in the background, pictures hanging, or a hole in the wall. These all are very distracting. Also, make sure that there isn't a door in the background. You may think nothing of it, but it can pull focus away from you. The casting director may be anticipating a grand entrance from a family member during your scene. You want them to be focused on you.

An ideal background for a self-tape audition is a solid neutral gray wall. Many classical portrait painters painted their subjects against a neutral gray backdrop. It made the colors stand out, and it's flattering to most hair colors and skin tones. It's important that you have enough room to create some space between you and the backdrop to avoid shadows (more on that later). The background should be smooth, so avoid using a sheet hanging from the wall. The wrinkles will be distracting. No matter how carefully you iron the sheet, you can always see the wrinkles, and it flutters with the slightest movement of air in the room.

If you have a smooth gray wall in your home, you may be all set. However, if you don't, another practical option is to purchase a roll of seamless photo background paper. You can purchase a roll online or in professional camera stores. They're very affordable and sold in rolls that are about 9 feet wide and 36 feet long. They have been a long-time staple of commercial and fashion photographers. Their neutral color focuses the attention on the subject and allows for versatile lighting. The best part is you can use painter's tape to tape it to the wall and roll it up easily for efficient storage. And it's long enough to share with friends! Another great option is to purchase a non-reflective, wrinkle-resistant fabric backdrop and portable stand. If you are self-taping a lot and have a designated space, this can be a wonderful option.

Chapter Notes
- Find an accessible space now.
- Make sure it is quiet, without an echo.
- Have a solid backdrop (preferably neutral gray), without furniture or pictures in the background.

24

LIGHTS, CAMERA, AND SOUND
BUILDING AN AFFORDABLE STUDIO

Lighting

Just Make It Look Good

I was fortunate to work with the brilliant cinematographer Brian J. Breheny, who received a BAFTA nomination for Best Cinematography for the film *The Adventures of Priscilla, Queen of the Desert*. One day, I asked him about lighting techniques. I was curious if he preferred three-point lighting or a different technique. I will never forget his advice, "Just look at it, and make sure it looks good." Good idea. Well, we might not all have the same eye as Brian, but his advice is something we should always consider when self-taping. Take a moment to really look at the lighting. If you love it, the casting director probably will too.

Natural Light

When you are selecting the space for your self-tape studio, pay close attention to the natural light. Does the space have a nice window that brightens up the room? If so, you may not need to purchase lights. However, if you are using natural light from a window, make sure that it isn't too harsh or bright. Ideally, you want diffused light that is consistent and does not over- or under-light you. Also, try to avoid self-taping when the light coming through your window is constantly shifting owing to moving clouds. This could dramatically affect your footage by creating moving shadows on your face, which will be distracting to the casting director. One way to soften the shadows is to diffuse the light source with sheer curtains. Run some tests with the natural light in your space during different times of the day. Play the footage back and see if you are too dark or too bright. Get creative, until you find your ideal lighting setup.

Studio Light

Inexpensive artificial light is great because it is easy to control. No matter what lighting system you use, you want to make sure that the light is coming from a big source and is diffused. This will create a "soft" look that is evenly spread across your face, without hard shadows. Your self-tape lighting should look cool rather than warm. Cool lighting appears more white or blue, and warm lighting has a yellowish look. You can purchase affordable LED lights that are easy to set up, and they will provide you with a professional quality. Some of the most popular options today, are LED softbox lights with dimmers, LED video lighting kits, or a ring light that conveniently fits around your smartphone. I prefer to use LED softboxes with dimmers, LED umbrella lights, or an LED video lighting kit. The quality is great, and they give you more shooting options. The LED softboxes do a wonderful job of softening the light. The ring light is affordable and easy for travel, but it has little versatility. It will often create a catchlight or reflection of the ring light in your eyes. An LED softbox or video lighting kit comes with light stands, and the brightness can be adjusted by simply turning a dial. I prefer the LED dimmable lighting kits that have a temperature range that varies from 3200K (warm) to 5600K (white). These are simple to use and easy to store. Regardless of the kind of LED light setup that you decide to invest in, the goal is to make the lighting sharp and professional.

For you filmmakers out there, you are probably familiar with a technique called *three-point lighting*: key light, fill light, and backlight. Three-point lighting is a great way to create a theatrical mood for a scene. However, for our purposes, a two-point lighting system will do the job. Remember, you want the light to be "soft" and evenly spread across your face, without shadows. So, place an LED light on each side of the camera, angled at about 45 degrees. You want the lights focused on both sides of your face and slightly above your eye-line. By the time this book is published, there will be new products on the market, but the principles of using light will remain.

No Shadows Please

Make sure that you remove the shadows from your face and from the backdrop behind you. You want the casting director to be focused on your performance, not the shadows. If your light is too bright or powerful, it will create hard shadows on the surface behind you. If you are too close to the background, you will see your shadow on the backdrop. If the light is placed too high above your head, angled down at you, you may have shadows under your eyes. So, make sure that your lights are placed slightly above your eyeline and pointed toward you. The easiest way to remove shadows from your backdrop is to move forward, a few feet away from your backdrop. When you create space between you and the backdrop, the shadows will begin to disappear. The closer you are to your backdrop, the harsher the shadows. If you are in a tight space, another way is to move one of the lights and angle it more to the side of your face. This will cause your shadow to move off of the backdrop, but make sure that you have enough light on the front of your face so that you are well lit.

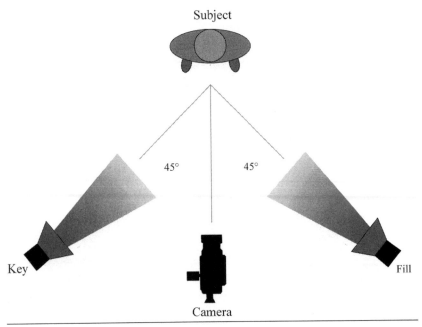

Two-Point Lighting Setup. (Photo by John James Hickey.)

Keep It Simple – and Cheap

There are many options for high-quality, affordable lights for your self-tape studio. If you follow the basic lighting principles and use some creativity, you will be on your way in no time. Keep it simple, make it look good, and start figuring out the lighting system that works for you.

Cameras

An expensive camera will not make you a great actor, but a good-quality image is important. Technology is moving at lightning speed, and it is amazing to see the quality in cameras that are available at an affordable price. You don't need to go out and purchase the newest Black Magic or ARRI Alexa camera for your self-taping needs. You can get a great camera without spending your life savings. It's important that your footage looks professional, but remember, the camera you use will not get you the job. Find the balance between quality and cost ... you may find the answer in the phone you are holding.

The Camera Phone

Most smartphones will work just fine. The quality on them is incredible and getting better every day. Even big-time directors are beginning to lean on the superb quality of the camera on cell phones. Famous director Steven Soderbergh has shot feature films on an iPhone: *Unsane*[1] and *High Flying Bird*[2]. I should mention, however, that those movies were shot with different lenses attached to the iPhone. For your purposes, the smartphone that you probably already own will do just fine.

Lens for the Smartphone

Buying a lens that you can easily attach to your smartphone is a wonderful option to improve the quality of your self-tape audition. There are many products available, and there will be more by the time this book is published. So, do your research and stay in tune with your options. As of now, I prefer the Moment Tele 58mm lens. It is easy to attach to your smartphone, and the 58mm lens will give your footage a more cinematic look. It will allow some distance between you and the camera. It will focus on the details of your face and put the background in softer focus.

Having an attachment lens will improve the quality of your footage and will give you more options when shooting.

DSLR Camera

If you want to up your game a little, visit a commercial store that specializes in professional video equipment. Talk to a specialist, discuss with them your specific needs, and ask them about purchasing a used camera. If you go to a major retailer, then you are guaranteed that all of their used equipment has been tested before resale. You can get some great deals. A 50mm lens on a DSLR camera will work best for shooting your self-tape audition in a medium close-up frame.

Sound

An audience can forgive a weak acting moment, a bad edit, an undesirable frame, but they will not tolerate poor quality of sound. Distracting sound will immediately make the casting director tune out during your audition. Good sound is vital for a professional self-tape audition, so definitely make it a priority.

Microphones for Smartphones

The internal microphones on most smartphones are not the best quality. I recommend purchasing a separate microphone. Lavalier or shotgun microphones are affordable options for your smartphone. The lavalier microphone comes with a long thin cable that attaches to your phone and can easily be run under your shirt and clipped onto to your collar. Another option is the mini-shotgun directional microphone that attaches right to the smartphone. It's wonderful for self-taping and allows you freedom when performing because it is not attached to you. Today, the two brands that I recommend are Shure and Rode.

Microphones for DSLR Cameras

Purchase a directional shotgun microphone that attaches to the camera. This will give you much better audio quality and is well worth the small investment. Rode makes wonderful shotgun microphones for DSLR cameras.

Tripods

Put it on Sticks

Always use a tripod (known in the industry as "sticks") when filming your self-tape audition. *Never do it handheld.* You may think that your friend has a steady hand, but they probably don't. It is very distracting to watch a self-tape audition with the camera shaking the entire time. So, get a tripod to lock your camera down and make sure that it can extend higher than you. You can purchase many affordable tripods. It's a small investment to take your self-tape audition to a professional level, and it will. I recommend using a tripod with a mount for the smartphone (if that is what you are using). It is much easier to get a level shot using a tripod with a built-in level, and it is well worth the investment.

Chapter Notes

- LED lighting kit or LED softboxes with dimmers work great.
- Two-point lighting angled at about 45 degrees is ideal for self-tapes.
- Remove background shadows by creating space between you and the backdrop.
- A smartphone (with a 58mm attachment lens) works great.
- A shotgun microphone works best because you can move freely without sound interference.
- Always use a tripod.

25

FILMING

SLATING, INTIMACY, PROPS, THE READER

Framing

The framing is very important for your self-tape submission. *Always record your audition horizontally or in landscape mode.* The standard frame for self-taping is a medium close-up shot. You want the bottom of the frame around your mid-chest, and the top of the frame slightly above your head. The camera should be at your eye level to create a good eye-line. Think of it like taking a "selfie" with a friend. You never put the camera way below and pointed straight up at you. This angle would look weird and unflattering. Instead, you reach out and put the camera at your eye level or slightly above your eye-line to create a nice angle. Your character should have natural movements but be sure to stay in the frame. Play the piece of pie and keep your focal points within the imaginary triangle.

Sit or Stand

You may sit or stand, depending on the character and circumstances of the scene. If you are seated, it will be easier to ground yourself and avoid excessive movement, which can be distracting. Of course, if you feel that you need to stand for the scene based on the character's situation, then go for it. However, you will need a tall tripod, or a mini tripod that is elevated and level with your eye-line. When standing, give yourself a "mark" with a piece of tape on the floor to help you stay in the desired frame. If you are seated, be sure not to move the chair after you have set the frame for your shot.

Settings

If you are filming with your smartphone, take a moment to adjust your settings to improve your footage. Shooting in 1080P at 30fps will create a quality image. Enable "flight mode" or "do not disturb" on your phone before you begin recording. You don't want your audition to be interrupted by phone calls, texts, or notifications during your recording. Also, before your shoot, test your audio and video by recording a 10-second clip. Review it to make sure that it looks and sounds great. And be sure to give yourself a few seconds of footage before you speak your first line and after you say your last line. This will allow you to trim the video exactly where you want in editing.

Slating

Today, the most common self-tape slate is to say your name, height, and the city where you are based. For example, "I'm first/last name, 5 feet 8 inches. New York City." You could also include the name of the character. If you have representation by an agent or manager, you can provide that in your slate if you desire. Pay attention to the instructions from the casting director, because they may be different depending on the needs of the project. Keep it simple and follow any specific guidelines that they provide for you. Remember that your slate is an introduction to the person who may hire you for a job. You could be working many hours, days, or weeks on set. This is an opportunity to show your ability and professionalism.

Good Energy

Your slate should be an introduction to you on a good day. Keep your energy moving forward when you give your slate but avoid being fake or over-the-top. Remember, this is your introduction to a complete stranger. Imagine sitting next to a stranger at a bus stop and suddenly blurting out,

"Hi! My name is Sam!" with ten times the energy needed to communicate a simple hello. That person would probably run away from you in fear. You don't want to make the casting director feel like that stranger; you want to be relaxed and genuine. It is your first impression, and it's important. This is your opportunity to grab their attention and share your personality. Imagine being the casting director watching 20 boring slates of disengaged actors in a row, and then your slate pops right out at them with your friendly personality shining through. This will make you instantly stand out for the right reasons, and they will remember you. Take a breath, enjoy it, and make it count.

Full Body Shot

Often, the casting director will ask you to submit a full body shot with your slate so they can see your physical build. After you slate your name, height, and city, have your camera operator pan the camera slowly down showing your physical build. After a beat, slowly pan the camera back up to your medium close-up shot and cut. You want to have the camera pan as smooth as possible.

Intimacy

If your character has physical contact or intimacy in the scene, you don't need to literally do it. If your character shakes hands with another character in the scene, you can give the feeling of shaking the hand by having a little physical movement and the way you deliver the line. If you have to kiss the other character in the scene, do not mime a kiss at the camera, unless you are attempting to create a comical moment. Instead, give the "feeling" of the intimacy by allowing the moment to affect your body and face. Take a moment where the kiss would occur and give the feeling of just having been kissed. Play the given circumstances of the moment, without the exact physical action.

Props

In general, don't use props in an audition, unless it is something that you would naturally have on you. For example, if it says in the script that your character is talking on their cell phone at the top of the scene, then use the phone that you have on you. If the script says that your character is working in a bar and walks up with a tray of cocktails, leave the martini glasses out of your audition and don't mime them. I once saw an actor audition for a popular dramatic television show. The character was a baker who was kneading dough in the scene. The actor wisely moved their hands, creating a small physical activity that gave the feeling that they were kneading the dough. It was simple and believable. Using a bunch of props in an audition can be distracting for the casting director. They are fully aware that this is an audition, so be believable and let them use their imagination.

Use Your Script

You can use your script as a universal prop. For example, if you are auditioning for a lawyer who is going over paperwork during the scene, use your script as the prop (but you should still know your lines). Using the script as a prop is a good way to give your character an independent activity and add dimension to your performance. It gives the casting director a subtle reminder of your creativity, and it adds believability to the scene. NYC actor Nicholas J. Coleman (*Orange is the New Black, Blue Bloods, Inside Amy Schumer, Billions, Law and Order: SVU*) offered this advice:

> I try to always have my script in hand – this is kind of a visual cue to the casting and producers that what they're seeing is an audition and not a final performance. Because I always memorize my audition sides, it's there mostly as a reminder, and not really for reading lines. So, where possible, I use the script as a replacement for in-scene props. I've used my script as a "clipboard" for medical scenes and a notepad for a detective. But you can also use it in other ways – the script doesn't have to stay a bunch of loose sheets of paper. It can be folded, rolled, or wadded up. By rolling the script into a tube, it can even become a gun for a scene as a soldier. There are a ton of creative ways to use the script as a prop, instead of it becoming a hindrance to playing the moment.

The Reader

If your audition is a dialogue scene between two or more characters, you will need someone to read the other roles for you off-camera. Call on your community of actors, so that you can help each other with your self-tape auditions. Support your fellow actors when they are in need of a reader, and they will be there for you when you need assistance. Build your team as soon as possible, and don't wait for the audition to arrive. The more times that you self-tape or help with a self-tape, the better your entire game will become. Think of these hours spent as training and fine-tuning your craft to *self-tape like a pro*.

Where Should the Reader Be?

The reader for your audition should be off-camera and not visible in the frame. Place your reader close to either the left or right side of the camera. Having them close to the camera will help create a good eye-line. If your reader is too far to the left or right of the camera, this will cause you to be in profile. The casting director wants to see your face and eyes, not your ear. Move freely, with natural movements, but play your angles (piece of pie) effectively. If you need a visual cue, remember to reach out and make a "V" or pie shape with your arms in front of you when you are looking directly at the camera across from you. The reader and your entire playing space are ideally placed when they are inside the "V" shape. This will help you maximize your performance on camera.

Two Off-Camera Characters

If your character is speaking to two off-camera characters in the scene, put them both within the "V" shape on each side of the camera. Ideally, you would want to have two actor friends available to read with you, but what if you only have one friend to read both of the characters? In this situation, imagine that one character is on the opposite side of the camera to your reader. This will make your performance look more believable. It will allow you to look back and forth across the camera lens creating a more dynamic audition. Be sure to rehearse, so that you are looking at the correct character each time. With a little practice, you will be amazed to see how believable you can make it appear that you are speaking to two characters with only one reader.

Not too Loud

Make sure that your reader isn't speaking too loudly right next to the camera. If you are using a shotgun microphone attached to the camera, the reader will be closer to the microphone and loud on the footage. In this case, have them speak quieter than normal. It is frustrating for the casting director when they have trouble hearing you because the reader is drowning out your performance.

Direction

Let's not forget to go *back to one* and take ownership of your audition! You've built your own self-tape studio and prepared the role. Trust yourself and go with your vision of the character. Give your reader direction. Tell them if you want to start the scene by looking away before they say their first line or if you want them to play a stronger action. Maybe you need them to take a *beat* in the middle of the scene so you can react to an important moment. The casting director always wants to see your interpretation of the character. So, make choices that get you excited to play the scene and collaborate with your reader.

Get Creative

Recently, I was on a vacation with two close friends. They have both been successful film/TV actors for over 20 years. They have been series regulars on many hit network television shows and have played large roles in Hollywood films. We were staying in a hotel, and the agent of one of the friends called her about an important audition for a role on a new television series. It was urgent, and she needed to get her audition in right away. I wish that I had taken a photo of our make-shift self-taping studio that day in the hotel. It consisted of a camera on a small travel tripod, sitting on a stack of books on top of an ironing board, with long thin curtains strategically placed to diffuse the light. She was seated on the hotel stool in front of a light-gray wall. My other friend and I read the roles off-camera, while he simultaneously ran the camera with his free hand. That day we got creative and made it happen. It was a fun moment that I will never forget. Sometimes, things aren't how we planned, but we must always find a way. Find your community, build your team, and support each other. And remember, when a friend of yours books a role, support them, because it is validation that you could be next!

Chapter Notes
- Frame yourself horizontally.
- Have the camera level with your eye-line.
- Adjust your settings before you record.
- The self-tape slate is your name, height, and city, delivered directly into the camera lens.
- Give the feeling of an intimate moment.
- Avoid using props unless it is something that you would naturally have on you such as a cell phone.
- Use the script as a prop.
- Have your reader next to the camera to create a good eye-line.
- If the reader is closer to the microphone, have them speak more quietly.
- Collaborate with your reader and make the audition your own.

26

EDITING AND SUBMITTING
IT'S AN AUDITION NOT A MOVIE

Editing

If you want to become a better actor on camera, learn how to edit. I cannot stress this point enough. Developing skills to become an average editor will instantly improve your performance on camera. You will begin to act with the editor's work in mind and understand what they need from you. When I learned how to edit, it changed the game for me. I have been fortunate to teach many actors how to act for the camera. I can testify that, once they learned basic editing skills, their work in front of the camera instantly improved. The difference between their performances before and after learning basic editing skills is remarkable.

Editing Software

Today, editing programs are user-friendly and easily accessible. There are many good editing programs that you can use, but I recommend Adobe Premiere Pro. It is professional editing software that is easy to learn. If learning computer programs is a challenge for you, ask around, and I bet you know many people that can teach you the basics of editing. There are wonderful tutorials on Adobe's website and YouTube. If you already have developed skills as an editor, bravo! You are ahead of the game. But, if you haven't, start learning how to edit now, or the business of acting may pass you by quicker than you think. You can sharpen your editing skills by using them on your self-tape auditions.

Edit on Your Phone

Remember when I started this part by saying that you are living in the most exciting time to be an actor? Everything is at your fingertips more than ever before. You can edit your self-tape audition right on your smartphone and then upload it to a platform such as WeTransfer or Dropbox. If you use an iPhone, you can edit your slate and audition on iMovie. What if you use an Android? Not to worry, you have plenty of options. There are many editing software programs available that you can quickly learn. As of today, check out Adobe Premiere Rush, KineMaster Pro, Filmora Go, WeVideo, and start practicing.

Submitting

Always follow the directions provided by the casting director on how they want you to submit your self-tape audition. Today, there are many different tools you can use to send your digital file. Currently, some of the most acceptable ways to submit your self-tape auditions are through a private Vimeo link, WeTransfer, and Dropbox. Submitting your audition file on Vimeo is a good option, but, if you do that, it's important that you always make the link private. Allowing anyone on the internet to see material from a film or television show before it has been officially released could compromise the project. A word of caution about links: with some companies that offer free service, the link expires after 7 days. That means, if the recipient doesn't view the file before the week has passed, the link becomes inactive, and the original files are deleted off the server. This could cause you to miss out on an important opportunity. So, always look at the fine print and consider paying for the premium or pro service to have more flexibility.

Separate Files

Casting directors usually prefer slates and auditions to be submitted as separate files. So, if you are auditioning with one scene, you can submit two files. If you are auditioning with two scenes, then you can submit three files. And, send your best take only.

Here is a standard format in which to submit your files:

Slate:
FirstNameLastName_ProjectName_CharacterName_SLATE.
mp4.

Scene #1:
FirsNametLastName_ProjectName_CharacterName_SCENE1.
mp4.

Scene #2:
FirstNameLastName_ProjectName_CharacterName_SCENE2.
mp4.

It's an Audition, Not a Movie

If you want to get a little more creative, you can edit your slate and audition together with a fade to black or a crossfade. Start with a black screen that has your name and the character name. Then, transition by fading into the audition and fading out at the end. If you have a slate and two scenes for the same project, you can edit them all together by fading in and out of each scene. However, this is your audition and not your short film. Be creative, but lean toward simplicity. With practice, you will find your own self-taping rhythm and style. But, remember to read the directions carefully. This is another opportunity to make a good impression by delivering your self-tape audition in the requested format. I hope that you will embrace the world of self-taping. Today, you have a lot of autonomy over your career. Strive to become the best actor you can be and keep developing your self-tape production skills.

Chapter Notes
- Learning how to edit dialogue scenes will improve your acting on camera.
- Find professional editing software that is right for you.
- Edit your self-tape audition on your smartphone.
- Follow the casting director's directions on how they would like you to submit your audition.
- Label your slate and audition files.

FINAL THOUGHTS

Why Do You Want to Be an Actor?

This book has been about *how* to act for the camera and pursue a professional career. However, it is important to always be in touch with *why* you want to be an actor. What is your specific *why* behind *what* you do? What sets your passion on fire? Obviously, this will not be the same answer for everyone. You must take time and address this deeper question within yourself. Is it because you want to become rich and famous? If it is, you may be disappointed. Or is it because you have a strong desire to express yourself creatively? Or is it because you have compassion for others? Or is it because you want to give a voice to characters that would otherwise be silenced? When you can answer this question, you will become unstoppable, and everything will fall into place. You will get knocked down, but you will get back up because you will know *why* you are continuing on. Acting for the camera is fun and exciting, but always be in touch with your personal mission statement. When you are, you will have the answer to any question that is presented to you. I believe in you, but what's more important is that you believe in yourself and know *why* you want to be an actor. When you have a deep reason *why* that burns inside of you, you will be on your way.

Create the Story You Want

"They succeed because they think they can."

—Virgil

Professional actors are artists who dream big, take action, and believe in themselves. They have victories and disappointments, but their passion is what drives their persistence. All of us have self-doubt creep into our minds, but, if you can clearly see your dream and keep taking action, I know that you will find success. However, you will find yourself in the company of people who will doubt you and say that your dreams are impossible. That's because your dreams are impossible ... for them. Stay on your own path and don't let others' fear define your story. You are the one creating your story. When I look at the careers of so many of my colleagues, it isn't always the most talented who have succeeded. It's those who are clear with their personal mission and who have been the most persistent. What about talent? How do we define it? Well, it depends on who you ask. Everyone has a different opinion on that. There are many successful actors working today who were not the "best" in their class. Focus your energy on being the best actor you can be and let go of the rest. Surround yourself with a team who supports you and enjoy the ride. Acting for the camera is an exciting business that can take you to places you never imagined. Be intentional with your goals and write out a plan to pursue them. Control what is within your control and just keep working. Every day, all over the world, there are actors working on camera, and there isn't any reason why you can't be one of them.

NOTES

Chapter 2.

1. Jory, Jon. *Tips Ideas for Actors*, Smith and Kraus, Inc., 2000.
   a. In-text citation: (Jory 3)
2. Davis, Viola, performer. *Fences*. Directed by Denzel Washington, final cut, Paramount Pictures, 2016.

Chapter 3.

1. Jory, Jon. *Tips Ideas for Actors*, Smith and Krause, Inc., 2000.
2. Davis, Geena, performer. Sarandon, Susan, performer. Pitt, Brad, performer. *Thelma and Louise*. Directed by Ridley Scott, final cut, Metro-Goldwyn-Mayer, 1991.
3. "Jack Nicholson preppin' for The Shining." *YouTube*, uploaded by Humpzilla21, 8 Mar., 2011. https://www.youtube.com/watch?v=Qu3xxq5F3Gw
   In-text citation: ("Jack Nicholson preppin'")
4. Nicholson, Jack, performer. Duvall, Shelly, performer. *The Shining*. Directed by Stanley Kubrick, final cut, Warner Bros., 1980

Chapter 4.

1. Teller, Miles, performer. Simmons, J.K., performer. *Whiplash*. Directed by Damien Chazelle, final cut, Sony Pictures (North America), Stage 6 Films (International), 2014.

Chapter 5.

1. "Aaron Sorkin: From Addict to Academy Award Nominee." *YouTube*, uploaded by CBS News, 6 Feb. 2011, https://www.youtube.com/watch?v= ObIfH4utYPU.
2. *Bridesmaids.* Directed by Paul Feig, Universal Pictures, 2011.
3. Lawrence, Jennifer, performer. Cooper, Bradley, performer. *Silver Linings Playbook.* Directed by David O. Russell, final cut, The Weinstein Company, 2012.

Chapter 6.

1. "Core Beliefs." *Stella Adler Studio of Acting*, https://www.stellaadler.com/about/core-beliefs/
2. DiCaprio, Leonardo, performer. Bracco, Lorraine, performer. *The Basketball Diaries.* Directed by Scott Kalvert, final cut, New Line Cinema, 1995.

Chapter 9.

1. Swanson, Gloria, performer. Holden, William, performer. *Sunset Boulevard.* Directed by Billy Wilder, final cut, Paramount Pictures, 1950.
2. Welsch, Tricia. *Gloria Swanson: Ready for Her Close-Up*, University Press of Mississippi, 2013.

Chapter 10.

1. Lyman, Rick. *"Marlon Brando, Oscar-Winning Actor, Is Dead at 80."* New York Times, July 2, 2004.
2. Caine, Michael. *Acting in Film*, Applause Theatre Book Publishers, 1990, 1997. a. In-text citation: (Caine 61)
3. Streep, Meryl, performer. *Sophie's Choice.* Directed by Alan J. Pakula, final cut, Universal Pictures, Associate Film Distribution, 1982.
4. Henson, Taraji P., performer. Cheadle, Don, performer. *Talk To Me.* Directed by Kasi Lemmons, final cut, Focus Features, 2007.
5. Henson, Taraji P., performer. *Hidden Figures.* Directed by Theodore Melfi, final cut, 20th Century Fox, 2016.
6. *Frasier.* Created by David Angell, Peter Casey, and David Lee, NBC, 1993-2004.
7. *black-ish.* Created by Kenya Barris, ABC, 2014 – present.
8. *How I Met Your Mother.* Created by Carter Bays and Craig Thomas, CBS, 2005-2014.
9. *The Office (American TV Series.)* Based on *The Office* created by Ricky Gervais and Stephen Merchant, NBC, 2005-2013.

Chapter 11.

1. *For Life*. Created by Hank Steinberg, ABC, 2020-present.
2. *Field of Dreams*. Directed by Phil Alden Robinson, Universal Pictures, 1989.
3. *Revenge of the Nerds*. Directed by Jeff Kanew, 20th Century Fox, 1984.
4. *The West Wing*. Created by Aaron Sorkin, Warner Bros. Television, 1999-2006.
5. *Thirtysomething*. Created by Edward Zwick and Marshall Herskovitz, MGM Television, 1987-1991.

Chapter 12.

1. Chalamet, Timothee, performer. Stuhlbarg, Michael, performer. *Call Me by Your Name*. Directed by Luca Guadagnino, final cut, Sony Pictures Classic, Warner Bros. Pictures (Italy), Memento Films International (worldwide), 2017.
2. Stevens, Sufjan. "Visions of Gideon". *Call Me by Your Name: Original Motion Picture Soundtrack*, 2017.

Chapter 14.

1. Hendricks, Christina, performer. Slattery, John, performer. "The Beautiful Girls." *Mad Men*. Created by Matthew Weiner, season 4, episode 9, AMC, 2010.

Chapter 15.

1. Washington, Denzel, performer. Hanks, Tom, performer. *Philadelphia*. Directed by Jonathan Demme, final cut, TriStar Pictures, 1993.

Chapter 17.

1. *Fall Time*. Directed by Paul Warner, performances by Mickey Rourke, David Arquette, and Stephen Baldwin, Capitol Films, Live Entertainment, Bates Entertainment, 1995.

Chapter 24.

1. *Unsane*. Directed by Steven Soderbergh, Bleeker Street Fingerprint Releasing, 20th Century Fox, 2018.
2. *High Flying Bird*. Directed by Steven Soderbergh, Netflix, 2019.

GLOSSARY OF FILM TERMS

Action   On set, it is the director's or 1st AD's command to begin shooting the scene. In script analysis, it is what a character says or docs to achieve an objective. They are playable action verbs that are selected by the actor.

Actor's demo reel   A 1–2-minute edited video featuring clips of an actor's best performances. Actors use demo reels to market themselves to industry professionals.

Actor's slate   The actor's introduction of themselves for an on-camera audition delivered directly into the camera. Usually, the slate will include their name, height, and what role they are reading for.

Automated dialogue replacement (ADR)   The process of re-recording dialogue in a studio after a scene has been shot to replace unacceptable sound quality. Also known as looping.

Back to one   A phrase used by the 1st AD to instruct the actors and crew to go back to their first positions at the top of the scene after a take is completed.

Beat   In script analysis, a beat is a smaller subdivision of a scene. A new beat occurs when there is a shift in subject in either the text or subtext between the characters. Beats can help actors analyze each section for comprehension, quickly memorize the text, and avoid playing results. In screenwriting, "(beat)" indicates a pause in the dialogue or action.

Appearing in parentheses between two lines of dialogue, beats usually indicate an internal change or shift in thought or emotion. Often, this is where the editor may cut for a reaction shot.

Blocking   The physical movement direction given by the director to the actor and camera operators to be performed in the scene. Positions are marked with color-coded spike tape on the floor.

Boom operator   Assistant to the production sound mixer who operates the boom microphone to record the dialogue in a scene.

Call sheet   A document that is sent out at the end of the day to the cast and crew containing details for the next day's shooting orders.

Camera operator   The person who operates the camera and executes the framing as directed by the cinematographer and/or the director.

Camera right or left   The direction of the actor's movements as seen from the camera. Ergo, an actor instructed to take two steps camera left will take two steps to their right.

Camera time   When the actor moves a little slower to allow the camera operator to move with them.

Casting director   The person who organizes all aspects of casting, including recommending actors, scheduling auditions, and completing the deal when the actor is hired.

Cinematographer or director of photography (DP)   Responsible for artistic and technical decisions about lighting and the framing of each shot.

Close-up (CU)   A tight shot that frames the face from the neck up.

Continuity   The process of ensuring the physical details and emotional content from shot to shot are consistent. The actor and the director are responsible for tracking emotional continuity. The script supervisor is responsible for tracking the physical details including set dressing, wardrobe, props, hair, make-up, and the actions of the actors during a scene.

Coverage   The series of shots (master, medium close-ups, two shots, close-ups, inserts, etc.) needed to tell the narrative of a scene.

Craft services   The department that provides meals for the cast and crew.

Cross-camera reaction   A reaction where the actor crosses the lens with their eyes to the other side of the camera.

Cut   The director's instruction to stop recording. For an editor, a cut is an abrupt transition from one shot to another. Also, a version of the film or show that was edited (e.g., rough cut, final cut, director's cut).

Day player   An actor in a supporting role paid by the day.

Depth of field (DOF)   The range of distance that a camera's subject will be in focus. A large DOF refers to a deep area of focus (i.e., both the background and foreground are sharp and clear). A shallow DOF refers to a small area of focus (i.e., the subject is in focus, and the background is blurry).

Director   The person in charge of the creative and dramatic aspects of the film who guides the cast and crew toward the execution of that vision.

Dutch angle or Dutch tilt   A camera angle first used by German (Deutsche) Expressionists in the 1920s where the camera is tilted on its roll or x-axis causing the horizon in the shot to no longer to be parallel to the bottom of the frame. Dutch angles are used to create a sense of unease or disorientation for the viewer.

Emotional continuity   The believability of your character flowing from one scene to the next throughout the story.

Extreme close-up (ECU)   A very tight shot focusing perhaps on just the eyes or lips.

Eye-line   The focal point where the actor is looking during a scene. Eye-lines help the audience understand who or what the actor is looking at. When a character looks off-screen or to a different character, the audience expects to see what the character sees.

First assistant camera (1st AC or focus puller)   Stands next to the camera and is in charge of keeping the subject in focus throughout the scene.

First assistant director (1st AD or first)   Manages the entire film. ADs work with the director and the cinematographer to break down the script and determine a shot list. They create the daily call sheets and track the daily progress against the schedule. Firsts are the liaison between the director and crew. They execute the "calling of the roll" – cuing the department heads (camera operator, key grip, sound mixer) to prepare for filming to begin.

First team   The principal actors.

Focal shift   When an actor shifts focus from one point to another. Focal shifts can help create a reaction or a cutting point for the editor.

Frame   The actor's playing space or picture that can be seen through the viewfinder on a camera and set by the cinematographer.

Given circumstances   Facts about the character and scene provided by the screenwriter. These include the location, time, and all present or past facts that affect the character in that moment.

High angle   When the camera is positioned high (such as in a tree) and focused on the actor down below.

Insert shot   Usually a close-up shot, that has the viewer focus on a specific detail in a scene (such as a letter, text message, or a ring).

Lavalier   A small body microphone that can be placed underneath clothing or clipped to the collar of a shirt.

Low angle   When the camera is positioned low (such as in a car trunk) and looking up at the actor.

Mark   The position of each actor indicated with a small piece of color-coded spike tape on the floor. "Hitting your mark" is landing on your proper position.

Martini shot   The last camera setup of the day.

Master shot   A camera angle that keeps all the actors in view and covers all of the action from the beginning to the end of the scene. Usually the master shot is the first scene shot for coverage.

Medium close-up shot (MCU)   A shot that is from the mid-chest up. One of the most common shots for an actor and the standard for self-taping.

Medium shot (MS)   A shot that is generally from the waist up. It gives the audience an opportunity to get closer to the character.

Motion capture (mo-cap)   Technology used to capture an actor's movements via electronic sensors on a body suit for the purpose of animating a digital character in a video game or a movie. It can also be used to capture the actor's subtle expression of the face or fingers and create characters such as King Kong, Gollum in *Lord of the Rings*, and George in *Rampage*. Also called *performance capture*.

Moving on   Completion of one scene and advancing to the next one.

Narrative description Describes the story within the screenplay. Written in the present tense, it includes descriptions of the setting, characters, and sounds.

Objective What the character wants from the other character in the scene. It should be simple, direct, and fueled by the emotional stakes of the character's circumstance.

Obstacles Anything that stands in the way of the character achieving their goals.

Overlapping dialogue When one actor speaks on top of another actor's lines. This is usually only done in a two shot or a wide shot. Overlapping dialogue limits the editor's options in a close-up or over-the-shoulder shot where only one actor's mouth is visible.

Over-the-shoulder (OTS) A two shot where the camera is placed behind the head and shoulder of one actor and focused on the person to whom they are talking. The back of the shoulder and head in the frame help orient the viewer and establish a connection between the characters. This is commonly used during a conversation between two characters.

Performance capture (PCAP) see *Motion capture.*

Physical continuity When the actor repeats the same physical actions for each take of the scene to help the editor to cut smoothly from shot to shot.

Pickup A portion of a scene to be reshot.

Piece of pie The imaginary triangle between the actor and both sides of the camera. The size of the shot dictates the size of the imaginary pie.

Point of view (POV) A sequence that is shot from a single character's perspective.

Post-production The period after filming has wrapped, when the picture and sound are edited, special effects are added, and the completed film is scored.

Rack focus (pulling focus) A filmmaking technique that shifts the focus (i.e., from one character or object to another) during a continuous shot. It is often used in a two shot where the actors are in different depths of field.

Reaction shot　A shot of a character thinking or responding physically while another character is speaking.

Relationships　The character's feelings toward the other character, themselves, and the location.

Scaling the performance　Adjusting the size of the performance dictated by the character, frame, and style of the story.

Scene heading　Screenplay format at the start of each scene that establishes the camera location (INT. or EXT.), the scene location, and time of day (DAY or NIGHT). Also called a slug line.

Second assistant camera (2nd AC)　In charge of giving actors their marks and operating the slate/clapper at the beginning of each scene.

Second assistant director　Assists the 1st AD with the call sheet, acts as a liaison between the actors and technical departments (e.g., hair, makeup, wardrobe), and directs the placement and timing of background actors (extras).

Second team　Actors who stand in for the principal actors while the crew sets up the lights and cameras.

Shot　The image that is recorded by the camera.

Shotgun microphone　An external microphone that is attached to the top of the camera, frequently used for self-taping.

Slate (clapper)　Two hinged sticks attached to a dry erase board that identifies each shot; sound synchronization is established by the sticks being clapped together. The slate is filmed before the start of each scene. If slating was not possible before a scene, the slate is filmed upside down at the end of the scene and is called a tail slate.

Spiking the lens　When the actor looks directly into the lens during a scene.

Subtext　The meaning that the actor puts underneath the line.

Super objective　The character's main goal throughout the entire script. It is what they are fighting for and drives their actions. Each scene objective for the character should add up to their super objective.

Take　Any recorded sequence of the scene.

Two shot　A shot with two actors in the same frame, often used to show the emotional relationship between the two characters.

Walk and talk A scene that is performed with the actors walking and talking throughout the scene while moving with the camera.

Wide shot A long, full, or establishing shot that shows the character or subject in their surrounding environment.

Wild lines Lines of dialogue recorded without picture for potential use by an editor.

Wrap When filming is completed for the day or the entire project.

INDEX

Printed in Great Britain
by Amazon

75112690R00115